"Being a world traveler, I can't help but drool when flipping [through] *[Fusion Food] in the Vegan Kitchen*. There's no reason why ethnic food [can't be] cruelty-free. Joni's new cookbook will become a staple [in my kitchen. Get] ready for a culinary adventure around the world."

—CHRISTY MORGAN, The Blissful Chef, aut[hor of *Bliss]ful Bites: Vegan Meals That Nourish Mind, Body, and Planet*

"*Fusion Food in the Vegan Kitchen* is a solid addition to a vegan (or veg-curious!) cookbook collection. Joni Marie Newman's recipes begin with the familiar, but with one or two interesting twists, she transports the cook to another country. Her recipe creations are perfect for your next vegan dinner party. The Indian-Spiced Pumpkin and Jackfruit Chili will be a new staple in this house!"

—JL FIELDS, co-author, *Vegan for Her: The Woman's Guide to Being Healthy and Fit on a Plant-Based Diet*

"From Spicy Korean Barbecue Jackfruit Tacos to Italian Grilled Corn, *Fusion Food* offers an inventive and unique take on global cuisine. Joni takes the best highlights of regional and ethnic dishes from across the world and puts them together in ways that only a talented and creative chef can master. Now we can pretend to visit two or three countries at the same time!"

—BIANCA PHILLIPS, author of *Cookin' Crunk: Eatin' Vegan in the Dirty South*

"Armchair travels have never tasted better! Innovative, fresh, and bursting with the flavors of the world, Joni Marie Newman's inspiring new book, *Fusion Food in the Vegan Kitchen* is a must-have for anyone who loves food. It's that simple!"

—COLLEEN PATRICK-GOUDREAU, bestselling author and creator of The 30-Day Vegan Challenge

"Welcome to culinary world harmony, courtesy of mix-master, Joni. Her ability to make seemingly disparate flavors play wonderfully together also serves as an important peaceful metaphor. Her Fusion Rice Bowl is my new go-to comfort dish."

—DYNISE BALCAVAGE, author of *Pies and Tarts with Heart*, *Urban Vegan*, and *Celebrate Vegan*, and blogger at urbanvegan.net

FUSION FOOD IN THE VEGAN KITCHEN

125 COMFORT FOOD CLASSICS, REINVENTED WITH AN ETHNIC TWIST!

JONI MARIE NEWMAN

Photography by WADE HAMMOND

FAIR WINDS
PRESS
BEVERLY, MASSACHUSETTS

© 2014 Fair Winds Press
Text © 2014 Joni Marie Newman
Photography © 2014 Rockport Publishers

First published in the USA in 2014 by
Fair Winds Press, a member of
Quayside Publishing Group
100 Cummings Center
Suite 406-L
Beverly, MA 01915-6101
www.fairwindspress.com

18 17 16 15 14   1 2 3 4 5

ISBN: 978-1-59233-580-0

Digital edition published in 2014
eISBN: 978-1-61058-879-9

Library of Congress Cataloging-in-Publication Data available

Cover and book design by Michelle Thompson | Fold & Gather Design
Photography by Wade Hammond

Printed and bound in China

This book is dedicated to those who dedicate their lives
to the betterment of the lives of animals—animal rights activists
and the farm animal sanctuaries. To the vegan bloggers
and cookbook writers. To the vegan shop owners and new
product inventors. You make the world a better place for the
animals, both human and non-. And for that, I thank you.

CONTENTS

INTRODUCTION
WHAT IS FUSION FOOD?

I was lucky enough to have been born in sunny Southern California, and am lucky enough to still live here to this day. One of the most amazing things about this place is the intense diversity of both the people and the cultures.

People from all over the country and the world gravitate to California for one reason or another. Maybe it's our breathtaking sandy shorelines along the mighty Pacific Ocean, or our close proximity to Mexico. Maybe it's the ability to go surfing at the beach in the morning, and then head to the mountains to snowboard in the afternoon. Maybe it's to chase a Hollywood dream. Or, maybe it's just simply for the warm sunny weather, which lends itself to long growing seasons and makes fresh produce available all year round.

Whatever the reason that people come, the result is a fortunate one: California is now a microcosm of the world, home to some of the most amazing and creative restaurants and cuisines ever.

If you want authentic Chinese, we've got it. Jewish deli? Absolutely. Korean? Indian? Ethiopian? Mexican? Japanese? Filipino? Italian? Peruvian? Brazilian? Vietnamese? Southern barbecue? Of course! Almost every town, big city, or suburb has just about every kind of restaurant imaginable.

Our diverse culture has also bred its own cuisine, known as California Fusion. California Fusion cuisine began showing its roots in the early 1980s as chefs began to focus on sourcing only fresh and local ingredients, and using those ingredients to reinvent traditional ethnic recipes. And we liked it! So much so that it's taken on a life of its own. Restaurants such as Michael's in Santa Monica, the Imperial Dynasty in Hanford, Chez Panisse in Berkeley, and Ma Maison in Los Angeles all pioneered the way for many others to mix and match ingredients and cooking styles from all over the world into new and interesting dishes.

But it wasn't just the ingredients that made these dishes so special. The flavors and textures just screamed *California*—lighter and fresher in style than their traditional (heavier) counterparts. And the special attention paid to presentation! Plates featuring perfect little towers of fresh produce, grilled or sautéed to perfection and drizzled with amazing sauces. A carrot never looked like art before!

As the years passed, the movement grew. And as the movement grew, more and more daring and delicious recipes were created. Now restaurants such as Red Hot Kitchen in Los Angeles and Dragon Loco in Ontario, and food trucks like Don Chow and Kogi, are bursting at the seams selling amazing fusions of American, Mexican, and Asian foods, from Korean barbecue tacos to sweet-and-sour burritos. Even American classics like hamburgers and hot dogs now have fusion upgrades.

But, what about us vegans? Well, that's where this book comes in to play. An entire book dedicated to vegan fusion cuisine! A book dedicated to scratch cooking. Dedicated to using fresh, local produce whenever possible. Dedicated to avoiding store-bought meat and cheese analogs whenever possible. Dedicated to celebrating the flavors of the plants, not hiding from them. And finally, a book dedicated to creating amazing vegan fusion meals that will leave you and anyone else you cook for (yes, even the meat eaters!) completely delighted and satisfied.

STOCKING A FUSION PANTRY

Cooking with ingredients from all over the world can mean you need a few new staples to add to your vegan pantry. Most can be found in any well-stocked grocery store or farmers' market, while a few of these can be found at either an Asian market or, as a last resort, ordered online.

Agar Flakes and Powder: Also known as *kanten*, this all-vegetable gelatin is derived from red algae. It is commonly used throughout Asia to thicken soups, desserts, and jellies. Most often, it is found in flake or powder form. If you search it out, you can also find it in sticks or rods that can be ground down to your desired consistency. To ensure the right amount gets used, I will always give the weight when calling for this ingredient in recipes.

Black Pepper: Freshly cracked is the only way to go! I recommend getting your hands on an easy-to-use grinder.

Chinese Hot Mustard Powder: This pungent powder is available online or at your local Asian grocer. Just add water, let it develop for about an hour, and voilà—hot mustard! S&B Oriental Hot Mustard Powder works well, but it can be very, very hot if you aren't careful.

Coconut Milk and Coconut Cream: Generally, when I call for coconut milk, I recommend the full-fat variety. It's usually found in a can in the international aisle of most grocery stores. If left unshaken, the coconut cream will separate from the coconut water. This thick, delicious cream is also called for in some recipes. Luckily, you can also buy just the cream!

Cola: Every now and again I call for cola (or root beer) in a recipe, for both moisture and sweetness. I recommend using all-natural colas, such as Hansen's or Blue Sky, because they use real sugar rather than high-fructose corn syrup.

Ginger: Fresh is always best, because its sharp, spicy flavor adds so much to whatever you are making. A little goes a long way, so I usually keep mine in the freezer to have on hand. Powdered ginger is not a good replacement for fresh, although it does have its own place in some recipes.

Jackfruit: This starchy fruit has a very mild flavor similar to a cross between a pineapple and a banana when ripe. When young and green, it takes on the flavors of whatever you cook with it. As it cooks, it breaks down into a stringy, almost meaty texture, which makes it a perfect medium for dishes simulating pulled pork or shredded chicken. It's almost impossible to find fresh, and when you do, it is almost always well ripened and too sweet for most applications in this book, so I stick to the canned variety, packed in brine (not syrup) for savory recipes.

Maseca: Instant corn masa is corn flour treated with lime. It is different than plain corn flour, grits, or polenta. There are several brands available, but Maseca brand seems to be the easiest to find and the most consistent. Recently I thought the packaging had changed and realized that there are two varieties, one specifically made for tamales, and one multiuse flour. I have used them both, with the exact same results. The difference is that the one specifically for tamales has a little bit of a finer mill than the other.

Mirin: A sweet rice wine for cooking, similar to sake but with a lower alcohol content, mirin can be found in the international aisle of most grocery stores.

Miso: This pungent paste has a variety of uses. Not only does it make a very versatile and simple broth, but also a little bit added to sauces, stews, and even cheese sauces adds depth of flavor and sharpness. It can be found in most Asian grocery stores, and sometimes in your local health food store (in the refrigerated section).

Noodles: Soba, spaghetti, macaroni, chow mein, rice sticks, orzo, penne—so many noodles, so little time! I call for a variety of them, most of which can be easily found in any well-stocked supermarket.

Nutritional Yeast: Ahh, the nooch. This flaky yellow yeast is usually grown on molasses. It has a nutty, rich, almost cheesy taste that adds flavor as well as a nutritional boost (hello, B vitamins!) to your foods. Be sure to seek out "vegetarian sup-port" formulas. Nutritional yeast can be found in the vitamin and supplement section of most health food stores.

Sambal Oelek: This is a thick and spicy paste made from chiles and garlic. I am partial to Huy Fong Foods brand, which is made right here in sunny California! Sambal oelek should be readily available in any well-stocked supermarket (look in the international foods aisle), but it is way less expensive at Asian markets, if you happen to live close to one.

Sesame Oil: This potent and flavorful oil is a must in any fusion pantry, and a little goes a long way. I almost always call for plain sesame oil, not to be mistaken for toasted sesame oil or black sesame oil, which are even stronger in flavor.

Soy Sauce, Tamari, and Bragg Liquid Aminos: These three ingredients can be used inter-changeably in recipes. It really is a personal taste preference. For those with gluten sensitivities, wheat-free tamari and liquid aminos are usually good choices. Bragg is also lower in sodium than traditional soy sauce.

Sriracha: This condiment is otherwise known as the best hot sauce in all the land. This is a hot chile and garlic sauce flavored with a touch of sugar and salt. It is named for the coastal city of Si Racha in Thailand. Once again, I am partial to Huy Fong Foods brand, known by its signature rooster on the bottle (hence its nickname of "rooster sauce").

Tempeh: Whole soybeans fermented and pressed into a cake, tempeh is considered to be healthier and less processed than tofu, with an earthier flavor. It is available in a wide variety of shapes and sizes. I try to stick with the plain variety. For those who find the flavor a bit too much to handle, extra-firm or super-firm tofu can usually be used as a substitute in recipes.

Tofu: I call for soft silken tofu in a lot of recipes because it makes a great base for creamy sauces. I also call for extra-firm or super-firm tofu in a lot of recipes where the tofu will be the main star of the dish. If you are lucky enough to live near an Asian grocery that sells fresh tofu, buy it! It is so much better than tofu packed in aseptic packages. When using extra-firm or super-firm tofu, it is always best to drain and press it ahead of time, to save time when preparing the recipes. One of the easiest ways to do this is to sandwich the block of tofu between folded kitchen towels or a few layers of paper towels and then place a heavy pan or book on top to press out excess moisture.

Vegetable Broth: Everyone has his or her own favorite brand of broth, and mine is Better Than Bouillon. It comes in several flavors: Better Than Chicken, Better Than Beef, and Vegetable. It is a small jar of bouillon paste that has fantastic flavor, and I cannot recommend it highly enough.

Vegetable Oil: I generally use canola oil, but I know many of you don't. I also use coconut oil quite often, but I understand it can be cost-prohibitive. Peanut oil is also a favorite when I am frying, because it has a very high smoke point. Unless specifically noted, use any mild-flavored vegetable oil you like.

Vital Wheat Gluten Flour: This flour makes home-made seitan a snap. No more rinsing the starch out of the flour! Make sure when purchasing this ingredient not to grab "high-gluten flour" by accident, because it will not perform the same way in recipes.

FOOD ALLERGIES
AND NOTATIONS

To help you find recipes that suit your specific needs, you will find the following notations next to the recipes that meet the following specifications:

○ **Quick and Easy**

Recipes that can be prepared in thirty minutes or less, based on the idea that you have intermediate skills in the kitchen.

○ **Low Fat**

Recipes that contain 3 grams of fat or less per serving. Recipes labeled as low fat also contain no added oil.

○ **Gluten Free**

I have done my best to label recipes that do not contain wheat as a listed ingredient. Please double-check ingredient labels.

○ **Soy Free**

Recipes that are free of soy. Please double-check ingredient labels.

○ **Nut Free**

Recipes that are free of nuts. Please double-check ingredient labels.

DON'T FORGET TO CHECK THOSE LABELS!

Throughout this book, I have done my best to mark recipes that are free of soy, wheat, and nuts. Unfortunately, in today's global market, allergens have a way of sneaking into our foods, so it is important to be vigilant when it comes to reading ingredient labels.

Those with celiac disease and others who must maintain a strict gluten-free diet should use extreme caution when preparing recipes labeled as gluten free, because some ingredients not normally associated with wheat, such as soy sauce, vinegars, flavor extracts, alcohol, and oats, can sometimes contain small or trace amounts of gluten.

CHAPTER 1

IT'S ALL IN THE SAUCE, BABY!
FUSION SAUCES AND CONDIMENTS

Seriously! A good sauce can turn an ordinary dish into a fantastic feast for the senses. Not only does a good sauce taste amazing, but it also looks beautiful as it graces the top of your plate, whether it be in an artful drizzle or simply poured into a bowl for dipping.

This chapter is full of fusion sauces that you can make in big batches and keep on hand to add sass to your salads, pizzazz to your pizzas, kick to your kale, and zest to your zucchini. They add color, intrigue, and depth of flavor ... umami, if you will. It's the sauce that leaves feasters wondering, "What was that deliciousness?"

So, read on and create your own sauces, dips, and dressings. Not only will they be used throughout this book as crucial ingredients, but they will also breathe new life and inspiration into just about anything you make.

CREAMY SESAME SRIRACHA SAUCE

◉ Quick and Easy
◉ Gluten Free
◉ Nut Free

JAPAN
THAILAND
USA

Also known as spicy sushi sauce, this delicious sauce is traditionally made by mixing mayonnaise with sesame oil and Sriracha. The easiest way to veganize it is to just substitute Vegenaise for the mayonnaise, but I made a pledge to write this book without the use of premade substitutions, so here is a recipe that is made from scratch! (Well, except for the Sriracha.) I really love this stuff. I use it on everything: tacos, burritos, salads, as a dip for veggies, plus anything else I can think of. I always keep a squeeze bottle of this handy in the fridge.

12 ounces (340 g) soft silken tofu

½ cup (120 ml) vegetable oil

¼ cup (60 ml) sesame oil

1 tablespoon (10 g) minced garlic

3 tablespoons (45 ml) Sriracha

2 tablespoons (30 ml) rice vinegar

½ teaspoon ground mustard seed

½ teaspoon sea salt

Add all the ingredients to a blender and purée until silky smooth. Store in an airtight container in the refrigerator for up to 2 weeks.

YIELD: 2½ cups (600 ml)

FUSION TIP

As written, this is a full-flavored, high-fat dressing. The consistency is meant to mimic that of an aioli (or flavored mayonnaise). Feel free to replace half of the oil with water or vegetable broth for a lower fat version.

CILANTRO LIME CHILE SAUCE

● Quick and Easy

MEXICO
THAILAND

This tangy sauce has just a tad of heat and a bit of nutritional yeast and cashews to up the umami. I like this sauce as a dip and as a salad dressing. It's also good mixed with rice, potatoes, and pasta.

2 bunches (85 g) fresh cilantro

2 fresh jalapeños, stem, core, and seeds removed

¾ cup (180 ml) olive oil

½ cup (56 g) raw cashews

¼ cup (60 ml) soy sauce or tamari

¼ cup (60 ml) lime juice

2 tablespoons (15 g) nutritional yeast

1 tablespoon (21 g) agave

1 tablespoon (10 g) minced garlic

1 teaspoon Dijon mustard

½ teaspoon smoked paprika

Add all the ingredients to a blender and purée until smooth. Store in the refrigerator in an airtight container for up to 2 weeks.

YIELD: 3 cups (705 ml)

FUSION TIP

For a lower fat version, substitute water or vegetable broth for half of the olive oil.

SARA'S PERUVIAN AJI SAUCE

○ Quick and Easy
○ Gluten Free
○ Soy Free
○ Nut Free

PERU

USA

My Peruvian friend, Sara, was the first to show me this delicious green sauce, but of course I had to make some of my own gringa variations! Aji amarillo escabeche peppers, also known as Peruvian yellow peppers or chile guero, are dark yellowish orange chile peppers from Peru that are about the size of a large jalapeño. Most likely found at a Latin market in the freezer, they are precooked and then frozen.

2 ounces (56 g) fresh baby
  spinach leaves

1 ounce (28 g) fresh parsley

6 aji amarillo escabeche peppers,
  thawed, with stems removed

1½ cups (355 ml) extra-virgin olive oil

2 tablespoons (20 g) minced
  garlic (about 6 cloves)

1 tablespoon (15 ml) lemon juice

salt and pepper to taste

Add all the ingredients to a blender and purée until smooth. Store in an airtight container in the refrigerator for up to 2 weeks.

YIELD: About 2 cups (470 ml)

FUSION TIP

For the gringa variation, you can substitute six whole roasted jalapeños for the aji amarillo escabeche peppers, and canola for the olive oil. If jalapeños will be your pepper of choice, leaving in the seeds or taking them out will be up to you. I like a spicy aji sauce (even as a gringa!), so I leave the seeds in. Remove the stems (and seeds, if not using) and place on a lined baking sheet and roast at 350°F (180°C, or gas mark 4) for about 30 minutes.

GARLIC ORANGE SAUCE

Rich with orange goodness, and as spicy as you like it by adjusting the amount of red chiles, this sauce works well as a dipping sauce, as a glaze for any of your favorite proteins, and over rice and vegetables, and is an essential ingredient in the Orange Tempeh Kebabs (page 39).

CHINA
USA

1 cup (235 ml) water

1 cup (235 ml) orange juice

¼ cup (60 ml) lemon juice

¼ cup (60 ml) rice vinegar

3 tablespoons (45 ml) soy sauce

2 tablespoons (12 g) orange zest

½ cup (115 g) tightly packed brown sugar

1 tablespoon (10 g) minced garlic

¼ to 1 teaspoon red pepper flakes, to taste

¼ cup (32 g) cornstarch mixed with ½ cup (120 ml) cold water to make a slurry

In a pot, stir together all the ingredients except the cornstarch slurry, and bring to a boil. Reduce the heat to a simmer and simmer for 10 minutes. Stir in the slurry and remove from the heat. Stir to thicken.

Keep warm until ready to use, or pour into an airtight container and store in the refrigerator for up to 2 weeks.

YIELD: 3 cups (705 ml)

CHIMI SAUCE

Traditional chimichurri is like South America's answer to Italy's pesto. Bright and fresh with parsley, lemon, olive oil, and garlic, it is primarily used for grilling meats. This sauce is a little bit South American and a little bit Southern California. The addition of sesame oil gives it a fusion twist, and this smooth blended sauce is as versatile as it is green. Use it as a salad dressing, dip, marinade, or sauce for burritos, or pour it over rice or pasta … the possibilities are endless!

2 bunches fresh curly parsley, stems removed and tightly packed (about 4 cups, or 240 g)

1 cup (235 ml) olive oil

½ cup (120 ml) red wine vinegar

¼ cup (60 ml) lemon juice

1 tablespoon (15 ml) sesame oil

6 cloves garlic

1 tablespoon (2 g) fresh thyme or 1 teaspoon dried

1 tablespoon (2 g) fresh oregano or 1 teaspoon dried

½ teaspoon smoked paprika

⅛ teaspoon chipotle powder

salt to taste

Add all the ingredients to a blender and purée until smooth. Store in an airtight container in the refrigerator for up to 2 weeks.

YIELD: 2½ cups (590 ml)

SESAME-GARLIC GINGER MISO DRESSING

This rich dressing tastes amazing over greens (especially kale!) and does wonders to wake up a boring, garden-variety salad.

1 cup (240 g) sesame tahini

1 cup (235 ml) water

3 tablespoons (45 ml) soy sauce

2 tablespoons (36 g) mellow white or yellow miso paste

2 tablespoons (30 ml) lemon juice

2 tablespoons (30 ml) rice vinegar

1 tablespoon (6 g) minced fresh ginger

1 tablespoon (10 g) minced garlic

Add all the ingredients to a blender and purée until smooth. Store in an airtight container in the refrigerator for up to 2 weeks.

YIELD: 2½ cups (590 ml)

SWEET CHILE SAUCE

Quick and Easy

Nut Free

CHINA

USA

Sweet and spicy, this sauce is great for dipping El Paso Egg Rolls (page 44), satay, or kebabs, or use it as a salad dressing. It is also a crucial ingredient in the Chinese-Style Macaroni Salad (page 59).

¾ cup (165 g) brown sugar, firmly packed

¼ cup (15 g) red pepper flakes (see tip)

¼ cup (32 g) granulated garlic

¾ cup (180 ml) rice vinegar

¾ cup (180 ml) vegetable oil

¼ cup (60 ml) soy sauce

Whisk together all the ingredients until well combined and the sugar is dissolved. Allow to sit overnight before using to allow the flavors to meld. Store in an airtight container in the refrigerator for up to 2 weeks. Shake before using, as the ingredients will settle.

YIELD: 1½ cups (355 ml)

FUSION TIP

Adjust the amount of red pepper flakes to taste; as written, this recipe is spicy, but not too spicy. However, if you are sensitive to heat, feel free to cut it way back, even as much as by half.

THAI PEANUT SAUCE

Quick and Easy

THAILAND

USA

This traditional Thai sauce adds a bit of fusion to anything you like, from Orange Tempeh Kebabs (page 39), to Korean Barbecue Satay (page 40), to drizzling it all over Thai Peanut Chicken and Waffles (page 90).

¾ cup (192 g) creamy, no-stir peanut butter

¾ cup (180 ml) water (add more or less to thicken your sauce to desired drizzling consistency)

¼ cup (60 ml) soy sauce

¼ cup (60 ml) sesame oil

¼ cup (60 ml) agave nectar

½ teaspoon ground ginger

¼ cup (25 g) finely chopped scallion or chives

1 to 2 tablespoons (8 to 16 g) red pepper flakes, to taste

Add the peanut butter, water, soy sauce, sesame oil, agave, and ginger to a blender and blend until smooth. Stir in the scallion and red pepper flakes. Store in an airtight container in the refrigerator for up to 2 weeks. It will thicken up in the refrigerator, so bring back to room temperature before using.

YIELD: Just over 2 cups (485 ml)

CREAMY CILANTRO PEPITA PESTO SAUCE

● Quick and Easy
● Gluten Free

MEXICO
ITALY

This sauce works well in so many dishes. It tastes great mixed with rice or over cold pasta for an easy pasta salad. Use it as a sandwich spread, or drizzle it over your pizza for an added zip. It is also a great salad dressing and dip for fresh veggies or pita.

1 bunch (42 g) fresh cilantro

5 cups (8 ounces, or 227 g) fresh romaine lettuce, roughly chopped (I like to use the inner leaves)

1 fresh jalapeño, seeded if desired

2 tablespoons (20 g) minced garlic

1 block (12 ounces, or 340 g) soft silken tofu

1 cup (64 g) raw pepitas (pumpkin seeds), without shells

½ cup (120 ml) olive oil

½ cup (120 ml) vegetable oil

¼ cup (60 ml) lime juice

½ teaspoon cayenne pepper, or to taste

¼ to ½ teaspoon sea salt, to taste

Add all the ingredients to a blender and purée until smooth. Store in an airtight container in the refrigerator for up to 2 weeks.

YIELD: 5 cups (1.2 L)

FUSION TIP

For a lower fat version, substitute water or vegetable broth for half of the oil.

SPICED KETCHUP

○ Soy Free
○ Nut Free

INDIA
USA

The heat in this sweet and spicy ketchup can be easily raised or lowered by adjusting the amount of red pepper flakes and jalapeño. As written it does have a bite, but it isn't over-whelming. I love this stuff with the Potato Mochi (page 32) and, of course, with french fries!

¼ cup (60 ml) olive oil

3 cloves garlic, cut in half

1 medium yellow onion, roughly chopped

10 leaves fresh basil, chiffonade

5 Roma tomatoes, quartered

1-inch (2.5 cm) piece fresh ginger, peeled and chopped

1 fresh jalapeño, stem, core, and seeds removed

1 teaspoon coriander seeds

1 teaspoon curry powder, store-bought or homemade (page 55)

¼ teaspoon ground clove

¼ teaspoon salt

¼ teaspoon black pepper

1 cup (235 ml) red wine vinegar

½ cup (115 g) brown sugar, firmly packed

½ cup (132 g) tomato paste

Heat the oil in a pot with a tight-fitting lid over medium-high heat. Add the garlic, onion, basil, tomatoes, ginger, jalapeño, coriander, curry, cloves, salt, and pepper. Cook until the vegetables are soft, about 10 minutes, stirring often.

Add the vinegar, brown sugar, and tomato paste. Stir to combine.

Bring to a boil. Reduce the heat to a simmer. Cover and simmer for 30 minutes, returning every 10 minutes to stir.

Remove from the heat. Allow to cool. Carefully transfer to a blender, or using an immersion blender, purée until very smooth.

Store in an airtight container in the refrigerator for up to 2 weeks.

YIELD: 4 cups (940 ml)

NORI GARLIC RANCH

Quick and Easy

Nut Free

JAPAN
USA

Doesn't the nutty seafood-y umami of toasted nori add such a great flavor to dishes? Ever since going vegan (it's been almost ten years now!), I have been adding seaweed to things to give them that little bit of flavor from the sea. This is no exception. The addition of ground-up nori flakes to this slightly kicky ranch is pretty fantastic. Use it as you would any ranch dressing or dip. On salads, with crudité, over tacos …

12 ounces (340 g) silken tofu, drained but not pressed

¼ cup (60 ml) mild-flavored vegetable oil

2 tablespoons (30 ml) rice vinegar

1 tablespoon (15 ml) agave or brown rice syrup

1 tablespoon (10 g) minced garlic

½ teaspoon prepared horseradish

1 tablespoon (2.5 g) ground toasted nori flakes (I used 2 sheets of toasted nori, ground in a dry food processor or coffee grinder)

1 teaspoon dried dill

½ teaspoon dried parsley flakes

½ teaspoon onion powder

¼ teaspoon sea salt, or to taste

¼ teaspoon chipotle powder or cayenne pepper

⅛ teaspoon ground cumin

⅛ teaspoon black pepper

¼ to ½ cup (60 to 120 ml) water

1 tablespoon (8 g) black sesame seeds

Add all the ingredients, except the water and sesame seeds, to a blender and purée until smooth. Add the water a little bit at a time until you reach your desired consistency: less water for a dip, more water four a pourable dressing. Stir in the sesame seeds. Store in an airtight container in the refrigerator for up to 2 weeks. Shake before using, as the oil and water tend to separate.

YIELD: 2½ cups (590 ml)

HOT, SWEET, AND SOUR SAUCE

- **Quick and Easy**
- **Low Fat**
- **Nut Free**

CHINA

USA

This sauce works well as a dipping sauce, tossed with your favorite protein to coat, and is an essential ingredient in the Hot, Sweet, and Sour Bean Balls (page 85); the Hot, Sweet, and Sour Seitan Ribs with Lemongrass Bones (page 88); and the Hot, Sweet, and Sour Cabbage (page 122).

2 cups (470 ml) pineapple juice

¼ cup (68 g) ketchup

2 tablespoons (30 ml) soy sauce

2 tablespoons (30 ml) lemon juice

1 tablespoon (15 ml) rice wine vinegar

1 tablespoon (15 ml) Sriracha sauce

1 teaspoon red pepper flakes, or to taste

¼ cup (32 g) cornstarch mixed with ½ cup (120 ml) cold water to make a slurry

In a pot, stir together all the ingredients except the cornstarch slurry, and bring to a boil. Reduce the heat to a simmer and simmer for 10 minutes.

Stir in the slurry and remove from the heat. Stir to thicken.

Keep warm until ready to use, or pour into an airtight container and store in the refrigerator for up to 2 weeks.

YIELD: 3 cups (705 ml)

PINEAPPLE TERIYAKI SAUCE

- **Quick and Easy**
- **Low Fat**
- **Nut Free**

JAPAN

USA

This salty sweet sauce can easily be made gluten free by using gluten-free tamari.

2 cups (470 ml) water

½ cup (120 ml) soy sauce

½ cup (115 g) tightly packed brown sugar

2 tablespoons (30 ml) agave

1 teaspoon grated fresh ginger

1 teaspoon crushed garlic

2 tablespoons (16 g) cornstarch mixed with ¼ cup (60 ml) cold water to make a slurry

¼ cup (40 g) crushed pineapple

Add the water, soy sauce, brown sugar, agave, ginger, and garlic to a sauce pot, stir, and bring to a boil. Slowly add the slurry and stir until thickened. Remove from the heat. Stir in the crushed pineapple. The sauce will continue to thicken as it cools. Store in the refrigerator for up to a week.

YIELD: 4 cups (940 ml)

MISO MUSTARD CHEESE SAUCE

○ Nut Free

JAPAN
USA

If you know one thing about me, you know that I love me some mac and cheese. This queso sauce is not only the main character in the Miso Mac and Cheese (page 93), but it is also a key player in the Not-Chows (page 116).

¼ cup (60 ml) vegetable oil

1 cup (160 g) finely diced onion

2 tablespoons (20 g) minced garlic

¼ cup (30 g) all-purpose flour

2 cups (470 ml) full-fat coconut milk

¼ cup (30 g) nutritional yeast

2 tablespoons (22 g) prepared Chinese hot mustard

2 tablespoons (36 g) mellow white or yellow miso paste

1 tablespoon (15 ml) soy sauce

1 tablespoon (15 ml) lemon juice

1 tablespoon (15 ml) sesame oil

1 teaspoon smoked paprika

To make an onion roux, heat the oil in a pot over medium-high heat. Add the onion and garlic and sauté for about 1 minute, stirring constantly. Sprinkle in the flour and stir to absorb all the liquid. (It should be the consistency of thick paste.) Continue to stir and cook until the roux is golden in color, about 2 more minutes.

Carefully add the coconut milk and stir until smooth and the consistency of gravy. Stir in the remaining ingredients.

Keep warm until ready to use, or pour into an airtight container and store in the refrigerator for up to a week.

YIELD: 3½ cups (822 ml)

SPICY KOREAN BARBECUE SAUCE
(see photo, page 14)

○ Quick and Easy
○ Soy Free
○ Nut Free

KOREA
USA

This sassy barbecue sauce has no tomatoes! It gets its red color from roasted red peppers that you can roast on your own, or use ones already roasted and packed in water.

3 tablespoons (45 ml) soy sauce or tamari

2 tablespoons (30 ml) sesame oil

2 tablespoons (30 ml) rice vinegar

2 tablespoons (30 ml) agave nectar

½ teaspoon powdered ginger

1 tablespoon (10 g) minced garlic

10 ounces (280 g) roasted red peppers

1 cup (235 ml) water

1 tablespoons (4 g) red pepper flakes

2 teaspoons (6 g) black sesame seeds

3 tablespoons (18 g) finely chopped scallion

Add all the ingredients except the red pepper flakes, sesame seeds, and scallion to a blender and blend until smooth. Stir in the red pepper flakes, sesame seeds, and scallion. Pour into an airtight container and store in the refrigerator for up to 2 weeks.

YIELD: 2¾ cups (650 ml)

CHAPTER 2

HORS D'OEUVRE, HORS D'OEUVRE?
SMALL BITES AND STARTERS

Have you ever seen the movie *Mermaids*? Cher's character, Rachel Flax, only knows how to make finger foods and appetizers, so that's all they ever eat. What fun! This chapter is full of small bites, hors d'oeuvres, starters, appetizers, and finger foods guaranteed to make Mrs. Flax proud!

PLANTAIN FRITTERS

These crispy fritters are so simple to make! I love to serve them as an appetizer with a variety of dipping sauces.

4 ripe plantains
¼ teaspoon turmeric
¼ teaspoon coriander
¼ teaspoon cumin
¼ teaspoon dried parsley
¼ teaspoon cayenne pepper
¼ teaspoon salt
⅛ teaspoon cinnamon
⅛ teaspoon cardamom
⅛ teaspoon powdered ginger
vegetable oil, for frying
nondairy sour cream, for serving (optional)

Peel the plantains and place them in a mixing bowl. Smash them until there are very few lumps. In a small dish mix together the spices. Add the spice mixture to the plantains and mix until well incorporated.

Pour the oil into a frying pan to a depth of ⅛ inch (3 mm) and heat to 350°F (180°C) on a deep-frying thermometer. Carefully drop ¼ cup (70 g) of the plantain mixture into the hot oil, and then flatten with the back of a spoon. Fry until golden brown, about 2 minutes, carefully flip and repeat on the other side. Transfer to a plate lined with paper towels to absorb excess oil. Serve with nondairy sour cream.

YIELD: 10 to 12 fritters (depending on the size of your plantains)

POTATO MOCHI (a.k.a. Japanese Potato Cakes)

• **Nut Free**

JAPAN

USA

These salty little cakes are coated in a glaze of soy sauce and rice wine. Use the optional nori wrappers as little handles for dipping! Serve with the Spiced Ketchup (page 23) or any of your favorite dipping sauces. This recipe was inspired by Kanako's Kitchen, www.kanakoskitchen.com, a website devoted to Japanese home cooking.

2 pounds (908 g) Yukon gold potatoes, peeled and cubed

salt to taste

½ cup (120 ml) full-fat coconut milk

½ cup (50 g) finely chopped scallion

¼ cup (32 g) potato starch (you can use cornstarch if you can't get potato starch, but cornstarch has a little bit of a grainy texture)

2 tablespoons (30 ml) vegetable oil, divided

¼ cup (60 ml) soy sauce

¼ cup (60 ml) mirin or rice vinegar

2 sheets toasted nori, cut into rectangles about 2 x 3 ½ inches (5 x 9 cm), optional

Add the potatoes and salt to a pot. Add enough water to cover the potatoes. Bring to a boil, reduce to a simmer, and cook until the potatoes are tender, about 10 to 12 minutes. Drain the water and return the potatoes to the pot. Continue to cook the potatoes over low heat for 2 to 3 minutes, constantly shaking the pot, to cause the potatoes to crumble and release excess moisture.

Remove from the heat and stir in the coconut milk, scallion, and potato starch. Mash together using a fork. Allow to cool enough to handle. Form the mixture into 14 patties, about 3 inches (7 cm) in diameter.

In a frying pan, heat 1 tablespoon (15 ml) of the vegetable oil over high heat. Add half of the patties, in a single layer, to the pan and fry until golden brown and crispy on both sides, about 2 to 3 minutes. While the cakes are frying, mix together the soy sauce and mirin.

Once both sides of the cakes are fried, pour half (¼ cup, or 60 ml) of the soy-mirin mixture into the bottom of the pan, making sure to shimmy the pan so that the entire pan is coated. Quickly flip the cakes so both sides get coated in glaze. Remove the cakes and place on a plate. As the cakes cool, they will firm up. If using the nori, wrap the nori around half of the cake. Repeat the process with remaining cakes and 1 tablespoon (15 ml) oil. Serve with your favorite dipping sauce.

YIELD: 14 pieces

POBLANO AND TERIYAKI SEITAN ASADA QUESADILLAS

● Nut Free

JAPAN
MEXICO

Serve these festive quesadilla wedges with a variety of dipping sauces. I love the Cilantro Lime Chile Sauce (page 17) and the Nori Garlic Ranch (page 24) with these!

4 large (10 inches, or 25 cm) burrito-size tortillas

½ cup (120 ml) Creamy Sesame Sriracha Sauce (page 16)

2 cups (60 g) baby spinach

1 recipe prepared Teriyaki Seitan Asada Strips (page 100)

4 large poblano peppers, roasted

1½ cups (270 g) Cotija-Style Tofu Crumbles (page 112)

Lay all 4 tortillas flat. Spread 2 tablespoons (30 ml) of the Sriracha sauce on each. On one half of each tortilla, layer one-fourth of the spinach, Teriyaki Seitan Asada Strips, poblanos, and tofu. Fold the tortilla in half to close the quesadilla.

Heat a dry frying pan or flat-top griddle over medium-high heat. Panfry each quesadilla until the tortilla is browned, 2 to 3 minutes per side. Cut each quesadilla into four wedges. Serve immediately.

YIELD: 16 pieces

FUSION TIP

You can add a bit of oil to the pan if you prefer a crispier quesadilla. Grill pans also make lovely quesadillas, complete with perfect grill marks.

JALAPEÑO CHIMI CORN SUSHI WITH CILANTRO LIME STICKY RICE

● **Low Fat**
● **Soy Free**
● **Nut Free**

MEXICO
JAPAN

Yep, Mexican sushi! This is a fun appetizer. I like to serve mine with a little dish of soy sauce and a healthy dollop of Creamy Sesame Sriracha Sauce (page 16). You will need a bamboo sushi rolling mat.

For sticky rice:

2 cups (360 g) dry white rice

2 tablespoons (30 ml) lime juice

4 cups (940 ml) water

1 tablespoon (15 ml) agave

zest of 1 lime

pinch salt

½ cup (8 g) chopped fresh cilantro leaves

For corn filling:

¾ cup (126 g) prepared black beans, drained and rinsed

½ cup (50 g) finely sliced leeks

1 roasted jalapeño, stem and seeds removed

1 cup (165 g) Chimi Grilled Corn (page 110), removed from the cob

1 tablespoon (15 ml) your favorite hot sauce (I like Frank's or Tabasco, or of course, my very favorite... Sriracha!)

8 sheets of toasted nori

To make the rice, add all the ingredients, except the cilantro, to your rice cooker and follow the directions on the cooker. Once cooked, let cool and then stir in the cilantro. This rice is very wet, almost pasty. Once it is cooled, it is very, very sticky.

To make the filling, toss together all the ingredients in a bowl until well combined.

To assemble the roll, lay one sheet of nori on your bamboo mat. Spread about ⅛ cup (30 g) of the sticky rice on the nori on the half closest to you. Add about ¼ cup (50 g) of the filling in the center of the rice. Using the mat, tightly roll the sushi—the tighter, the better (this makes it easier to cut). Use your fingertips to seal the edge with a little bit of water. Repeat with the remaining nori sheets. Cut each roll into 8 equal pieces.

YIELD. 8 rolls (64 pieces)

BARBECUE BUN PULL-APART BREAD

KOREA
USA

Not only are these buns a great play on a traditional steamed barbecue pork bun, but also the method used here will work wonderfully with all sorts of different fillings!

1 envelope (¼ ounce, or 7 g, or 1¾ teaspoons) active dry yeast

1 teaspoon sugar

½ cup (120 ml) warm water

2 cups (240 g) all-purpose flour

½ cup (72 g) vital wheat gluten flour

½ teaspoon plus ⅛ teaspoon salt, divided

½ cup (120 ml) water

1 tablespoon (15 ml) olive oil, plus more for brushing

1 heaping cup (250 g) prepared Spicy Korean Barbecue Jackfruit (page 96)

⅛ teaspoon onion powder

⅛ teaspoon garlic powder

⅛ teaspoon smoked paprika

⅛ teaspoon dried parsley

Mix together the yeast, sugar, and warm water. Let stand for 10 minutes.

In a mixing bowl, mix together the flours and ½ teaspoon salt. Add the yeast mixture, water, and 1 tablespoon (15 ml) olive oil. Knead for about 10 minutes, adding more all-purpose flour if the dough is too wet, or more water if it is too dry, a little bit at a time. Your goal is a soft, elastic dough that is easy to handle and not sticky. Form into a ball. Brush with a light coat of olive oil, cover with plastic wrap, and let rise for 1 hour.

Preheat the oven to 350°F (180°C, or gas mark 4). Have ready a 9-inch (23 cm) round baking dish.

Punch down the dough and knead for 2 to 3 minutes. Divide into 16 equal portions. Dip your fingers in olive oil, and flatten one portion of dough. Add 1 heaping tablespoon (16 g) of Spicy Korean Barbecue Jackfruit to the center and pinch the edges closed. Twist together the ends, and place seam side down in the baking dish. Repeat with the remaining 15 pieces, and fit them snugly into the dish, so they are all touching. Brush the entire top liberally with olive oil.

Mix together the onion powder, garlic powder, remaining ⅛ teaspoon salt, paprika, and parsley. Sprinkle the spice mixture evenly over the top. Bake for 25 to 30 minutes, until golden and firm to the touch.

Remove from the oven and allow to cool for about 10 minutes before pulling apart to enjoy!

YIELD: 16 pieces

BAKED AVOCADO FRIES

● Quick and Easy
● Soy Free
● Nut Free

These little buggers taste great on their own, but I actually love them as the main component of a taco. Put two wedges in a small corn tortilla, top with shredded cabbage and a squirt of Creamy Sesame Sriracha Sauce (page 16), and... tacos!

JAPAN
USA

½ cup (40 g) panko-style bread crumbs

1 teaspoon garlic powder

½ teaspoon paprika

½ teaspoon dried parsley

½ teaspoon dried dill

¼ teaspoon salt

¼ teaspoon black pepper

¼ teaspoon chili powder (for a spicier fry, use cayenne instead!)

¼ teaspoon dried oregano

4 ripe but firm avocados

olive oil spray (optional)

Preheat the oven to 350°F (180°C, or gas mark 4). Line a baking sheet with parchment paper or a nonstick baking mat.

In a small, shallow dish, mix together the bread crumbs and spices.

Cut each avocado into 8 wedges and dredge in the panko spice mixture. Arrange in a single layer on the baking sheet. For a crispier fry, spray with some olive oil. Bake for 20 minutes, flipping halfway through, and spray a little more oil. Serve hot.

YIELD: 32 pieces

SESAME TEMPURA VEGETABLES

JAPAN
USA

Crispy, with a hint of heat on the outside, and veggie goodness on the inside, these tempura vegetables are perfect with your favorite dipping sauce. Use this batter to fry up asparagus, broccoli, avocados, and sweet potatoes.

oil for frying

1 cup (120 g) all-purpose flour

1 tablespoon (8 g) cornstarch

¼ teaspoon salt, or to taste

1 teaspoon black sesame seeds

2 tablespoons (30 ml) sesame oil

1 teaspoon Sriracha sauce

1 cup (235 ml) club soda

18 to 24 pieces assorted vegetables cut into bite-size pieces

Add ¼ inch (6 mm) of oil to the bottom of a sturdy pan and heat to 350°F (180°C).

Add the flour, cornstarch, salt, and sesame seeds to a bowl and mix to combine. Add the sesame oil, Sriracha, and club soda and stir to mix until the bubbles from the soda subside.

Fully coat a vegetable piece in the batter and transfer to the hot oil. Fry until golden and crispy, flip, and repeat—about 1 to 2 minutes per side. Transfer to a plate lined with paper towels to absorb excess oil. Serve immediately.

YIELD: 18 to 24 pieces

ORANGE TEMPEH KEBABS

● Nut Free

CHINA
USA

I like to make these with just a few pieces on each skewer and serve them as appetizers with soy sauce for dipping, because they do well at room temperature. If you find tempeh to be a tad bitter, or you just don't like it, feel free to use extra-firm tofu (drained and pressed) instead. You can also steam or simmer your tempeh for about 20 minutes to really cut the bitterness. You will need 10 to 12 skewers.

1 pound (454 g) tempeh, cut into 1-inch (2.5 cm) cubes

½ cup (120 ml) orange juice

⅓ cup (80 ml) vegetable oil

¼ cup (60 ml) soy sauce or tamari

1 tablespoon (15 ml) ume plum vinegar or rice vinegar

1 tablespoon (6 g) orange zest, divided

¼ teaspoon red pepper flakes

1 cup (235 ml) Garlic Orange Sauce (page 19), divided

1 tablespoon (6 g) chopped chives

Place cubed tempeh in a bowl.

In a small bowl, whisk together the orange juice, vegetable oil, soy sauce, vinegar, half of the orange zest, and the red pepper flakes. Pour the marinade over the tempeh, and allow to marinate for at least an hour and up to overnight in the refrigerator.

Preheat a grill or grill pan to medium-high heat.

When ready to cook, thread 4 or 5 cubes onto each of 10 to 12 skewers. Brush each skewer with a coating of Garlic Orange Sauce. Grill each side for 3 to 5 minutes. The sugars in the sauce and marinade will caramelize and blacken. Continue to brush with the sauce until finished cooking. Finish with a final brush of sauce once removed from the grill.

Transfer to a serving plate, sprinkle with the remaining 1½ teaspoons (3 g) orange zest and the chives, and serve.

YIELD: 10 to 12 skewers

KOREAN BARBECUE SATAY

● **Low Fat**
● **Nut Free**

KOREA
THAILAND

Satay is a popular Indonesian street food, usually made up of different types of marinated meats and served with sauce for dipping. This version uses tofu marinated in the Spicy Korean Barbecue Sauce, then grilled up and served with a variety of dipping sauces. They are super easy to make and great as an appetizer at parties (or on game day!). You'll need 18 to 24 bamboo or reusable skewers.

1 block (1 pound, or 454 g) extra-firm or super-firm tofu, drained and pressed

1 cup (235 ml) Spicy Korean Barbecue Sauce (page 26)

Cut the block of tofu into thin strips that measure about 1-inch wide x ¼-inch thick (2.5 cm x 6 mm) and the length of the block of tofu (usually about 4 inches, or 10 cm). Place the tofu strips in a shallow dish or resealable plastic bag, and cover with the sauce. Marinate overnight in the refrigerator.

Preheat a grill or grill pan to medium-high heat.

When ready to cook, thread each strip lengthwise onto 18 to 24 skewers. Grill for about 5 minutes per side, or until you get no resistance when flipping. The tofu will stick to the grill until it is ready to be flipped.

Arrange on a plate with a variety of sauces for dipping.

YIELD: 18 to 24 pieces

SPICY SEITAN POT STICKERS

● Nut Free

MEXICO
CHINA

These little dumplings are a fun appetizer. They really satisfy my salty, spicy, savory cravings. I love to serve them with a variety of dipping sauces, including simply soy sauce! Another way to serve them is floating in your favorite broth. They can be made ahead of time and frozen for easy reheating later, too.

1 recipe prepared Sesame-Sriracha Seitan Crumbles (page 90)

½ cup (90 g) Cotija-Style Tofu Crumbles (page 112)

2 tablespoons (12 g) finely chopped chives

1 package (36 pieces) vegan pot sticker wrappers

oil, for sautéing (optional)

Toss together the seitan crumbles, tofu crumbles, and chives in a small mixing bowl until well incorporated.

Lay one wrapper on a flat surface. Add 1 teaspoon of the filling to the center of the wrapper. Dip your fingertips in water and run the water around the edge of the wrapper. Fold the wrapper over, into a half-moon shape, and press the edges together to seal. You can also use a fork to crimp the edges if desired. Repeat with remaining thirty-five wrappers and filling. Coat with a thin layer of oil.

Add the pot stickers in a single layer to a steamer, and steam for 10 minutes, or until hot and moist. They can also be sautéed in a bit of vegetable oil until golden and crispy, if desired. Serve immediately, or freeze for later use.

YIELD: 36 pieces

EL PASO EGG ROLLS

CHINA
MEXICO
USA

This Southwestern spin on a Chinese classic is a great appetizer or snack. I love to make up a big batch and leave them out on the counter to graze on throughout the evening.

2 cups (380 g) brown rice, white rice, or another favorite grain

1 cup (100 g) chopped scallion

1 cup (154 g) corn kernels

1 ½ cups (378 g) prepared black beans, drained and rinsed

2 fresh jalapeño peppers, core and seeds removed, finely diced

2 ripe avocados, mashed

¼ cup (4 g) chopped cilantro

¼ cup (60 ml) Creamy Sesame Sriracha Sauce (page 16)

1 tablespoon (10 g) minced garlic

½ teaspoon black pepper

½ teaspoon salt

¼ teaspoon ground cumin

¼ teaspoon dried oregano

20 (8-inch, or 20 cm) vegan spring roll wrappers

oil, for brushing or frying

Prepare your rice (or grains) according to the package instructions.

While the rice is cooking, prepare the filling. In a mixing bowl, add all the ingredients except the wrappers. When the rice is ready, add to the mixing bowl and mix until well incorporated.

Place ¼ cup (71 g) of filling in the center of one wrapper toward the bottom edge and wrap up like a burrito, using water to seal the edges.

These can be fried or baked. Of course, I like them better fried, but I know many people are more health conscious, so feel free to bake them.

If baking, preheat the oven to 350°F (180°C, or gas mark 4) and line a baking sheet with parchment paper or a baking mat. Place the egg rolls on the baking sheet in a single layer. Brush lightly with oil or spray lightly with cooking oil. Bake for 30 minutes, flipping halfway through, or until crisp.

If frying, preheat about ½ inch (1.3 cm) of oil in a frying pan. Carefully add 2 or 3 egg rolls to the pan at a time, and fry until golden and crispy on each side, about 2 to 3 minutes per side, then transfer to a tray lined with paper towels to absorb excess oil. Bring the oil back up to temperature and repeat with the remaining rolls.

Serve with your choice of dipping sauces or a sampler of a few different sauces. I highly recommend the Creamy Sesame Sriracha Sauce (page 16), the Sweet Chile Sauce (page 21), and the Nori Garlic Ranch (page 24).

YIELD: 20 pieces

BREAD PAKORA (Savory French Toast Dippers)

These dippers are a fun appetizer, but I actually love them for breakfast, served with Spiced Ketchup (page 23), Nori Garlic Ranch (page 24), and maybe even some maple syrup!

INDIA
USA

oil, for frying

1 cup (120 g) all-purpose flour

1 tablespoon (2 g) dried parsley

1 teaspoon garlic powder

1 teaspoon onion powder

½ teaspoon salt

¼ teaspoon baking powder

¼ teaspoon baking soda

1 cup (235 ml) unsweetened almond milk

½ cup (8 g) chopped fresh cilantro

1 artisan loaf hearty French bread (stale bread works well here, too)

nutritional yeast, for sprinkling

Add the oil to the bottom of a frying pan to a depth of ¼ inch (6 mm). If you have a deep-fat fryer, this is a great time to use it. Preheat the oil to 350°F (180°C) on a deep-frying thermometer.

In a shallow dish, mix together the flour, parsley, garlic powder, onion powder, salt, baking powder, and baking soda. Add the almond milk and stir to combine until there are virtually no lumps. Fold in the cilantro.

Cut the bread into strips about 4- to 6-inches (10 to 15 cm) long and 1-inch (2.5 cm) thick and wide. Coat each strip of bread with batter and place in the oil using tongs. If using a deep-fat fryer, it should only take 5 to 10 seconds to get nice and golden and crispy. If using a frying pan, fry on one side for 5 to 10 seconds, flip, and repeat until all sides are golden and crispy. Transfer to a plate lined with paper towels to absorb excess oil.

Serve sprinkled with nutritional yeast and your favorite sauces for dipping.

YIELD: 12 to 16 dippers

LUMPIYANG SHANGHAI

● Nut Free

The earthy, meaty flavor of the mushrooms fills in nicely for the traditional beef or pork usually found in this Filipino-inspired savory fried pastry.

PHILIPPINES
USA

2 tablespoons (30 ml) vegetable oil, plus more for frying

10 ounces (280 g) cremini mushrooms, finely chopped

1 cup (160 g) diced white or yellow onion

1 tablespoon (10 g) minced garlic

pinch of salt and pepper

2 cups (470 ml) beef-flavored vegetable broth (I really love Better than Beef bouillon in this!)

2 cups (140 g) finely shredded cabbage

1 cup (133 g) green peas

1 cup (108 g) shredded carrot

¼ cup (30 g) nutritional yeast

1 teaspoon dried parsley or 1 tablespoon (4 g) fresh, chopped

10 to 12 (8-inch, or 20 cm) vegan spring roll wrappers

Heat the 2 tablespoons (30 ml) oil in a pot over medium-high heat. Add the mushrooms, onion, garlic, salt, and pepper and sauté until the mushrooms have reduced in size by half and the onions are fragrant and translucent. Stir in the broth, cabbage, peas, carrot, nutritional yeast, and parsley. Bring to a boil, reduce to a simmer, and simmer for 25 to 30 minutes, stirring occasionally, until most of the liquid has been absorbed. Remove from the heat.

Lay one wrapper on a flat surface. Add ¼ cup (56 g) of filling to the wrapper, near the edge closest to you. Fold over 1 inch (2.5 cm) of both the left and the right edges toward the center. Roll up like a burrito. Seal the seam with water. Repeat with the remaining wrapper and filling.

In a frying pan, add oil to a depth of ¼ inch (6 mm) and heat to 350°F (180°C). Add 2 or 3 rolls to the oil and fry for 3 to 4 minutes, until golden brown and crispy. Flip and repeat on the other side. Transfer to a plate lined with paper towels to absorb excess oil. Repeat until all of the rolls are fried. Serve with your favorite dipping sauce.

YIELD: 10 to 12 pieces

MUSHROOM SPANAKOPENADAS

GREECE
MEXICO

Part spanakopita and part empanada, these triangles are a super-fun appetizer to have at parties and bring to potlucks because they taste awesome warm or at room temperature.

For mushroom filling:

½ cup (120 ml) olive oil, divided

8 ounces (227 g) button or cremini mushrooms, chopped

1 medium yellow onion, diced

3 cloves garlic, minced

½ cup (60 g) walnut pieces

½ cup (56 g) cashew pieces

¼ teaspoon cardamom

¼ teaspoon cinnamon

¼ teaspoon paprika

1 teaspoon garam masala

¼ cup (30 g) pine nuts

sea salt and fresh cracked pepper, to taste

1 package (16 ounces, or 454 g) phyllo dough, thawed according to package instructions

To make the filling, heat 2 tablespoons (30 ml) of the oil in a skillet over medium-high heat and add the mushrooms, onions, and garlic. Sauté for 5 to 7 minutes, or until fragrant and the mushrooms have reduced in size by about half.

Add the walnuts, cashews, cardamom, cinnamon, paprika, and garam masala to a food processor and pulse so that the mixture is chopped yet still chunky. Fold in the pine nuts and salt and pepper to taste.

Preheat the oven to 350°F (180°C, or gas mark 4). Line a baking sheet. Have waxed paper and a clean damp (not wet) kitchen towel at the ready.

Unroll the thawed sheets of dough. Place 2 sheets of phyllo on top of one another, keeping the remaining sheets covered with waxed paper and the damp dish towel, and cut in half lengthwise. Pile the sheets again on top of one another, and again cut in half lengthwise. This will give you 8 strips about 3 x 17-inches (7.5 x 42.5 cm) long. Repeat with the remaining 4 sheets of phyllo.

Place one strip in front of you. Lightly brush with remaining oil. Place another strip on top and brush with more oil. Place 1 heaping tablespoon (16 g) of filling in the lower corner of the phyllo. Fold the corner of phyllo over to enclose the filling and form a triangle. Continue folding (like a flag), maintaining the triangle shape. Put the triangle, seam-side down, on the prepared baking sheet and brush the top with more oil. Repeat with the remaining seventeen rectangles of phyllo and the filling.

Bake for 10 to 12 minutes, until golden and puffy.

YIELD: 18 triangles

THAI-STUFFED POTATO SKINS

THAILAND
USA

A crispy boat of hollowed-out potato filled with an unlimited variety of ingredients, usually bacon, cheese, sour cream, and chives: the beloved appetizer of bars and diners everywhere. These skins are way more fun! They are also great to prepare in advance. You can follow the instructions to make the skins only, and freeze or store them until you are ready to make them. You really can fill them with anything; I just happen to love potatoes and peanut sauce, so there's that.

For skins:

4 russet potatoes

¼ cup (60 ml) vegetable oil, divided

salt to taste

For filling

reserved potato

1 cup (30 g) baby spinach leaves, chiffonade

½ cup (56 g) cashew pieces

¼ cup (85 g) shelled edamame

½ cup (120 ml) Thai Peanut Sauce (page 19), plus more for serving

¼ cup (25 g) chopped scallion

1 teaspoon black or white sesame seeds

Preheat the oven to 400°F (200°C, or gas mark 6).

Rub the potatoes with some of the oil and bake for 60 minutes on a roasting rack, or directly on the rack of your oven. Remove from the oven and allow to cool enough to handle. Cut the potatoes in half lengthwise. Scoop out the flesh of the potatoes, leaving about ⅛ inch (3 mm) of flesh remaining. Place the scooped-out flesh in a bowl to use for the filling.

Raise the oven temperature to 450°F (230°C, or gas mark 8), or set to broil.

Brush or rub the hollowed-out skins with the remaining oil, inside and out. Place the oiled skins on a roasting rack, skin side down, sprinkle with salt to taste, and broil for 10 minutes. Carefully flip so the skin side is up, and broil for an additional 10 minutes. The skins should be browned around the edges and crispy. Remove from the oven and allow to cool enough to handle.

While the skins are cooling, make the filling. To the bowl with the reserved potato flesh, add the spinach, cashews, edamame, and the ½ cup (120 ml) Thai Peanut Sauce and smash together until well incorporated. Stuff each skin with the filling. Broil for 5 minutes, or until heated all the way through. Top with the scallion and sesame seeds and serve with additional sauce for dipping.

YIELD: 8 pieces

CHAPTER 3

MÉLANGE IN A BOWL
SOUPS AND SALADS

Nothing beats a bowl full of goodness, whether it's a salad to start off your meal or a hearty bowl of soup to cuddle up with on the couch. This chapter is full of recipes for salads, soups, chilis, and other fun stuff to pile into a bowl and get on it.

SWEET AND SPICY
CILANTRO-CUCUMBER SALAD

This simple salad works well as a side dish, or tossed into a green salad, thrown into a wrap, or added to a falafel or sandwich. The spice level can easily be adjusted depending on the type of peppers you use. The recipe calls for Fresno peppers. Fresno peppers are similar in taste and size to a jalapeños, but have much thinner walls. Young green Fresnos are mild, and red ones are much spicier. These peppers are native to California, so feel free to substitute jalapeños or serranos if you like it spicy, or even red bell peppers to keep it much, much milder.

3 cucumbers

4 Fresno chiles, seeded and finely diced

½ cup (8 g) chopped cilantro

¼ cup (60 ml) rice vinegar

2 tablespoons (30 ml) agave

2 tablespoons (30 ml) lime juice

1 teaspoon to 1 tablespoon (4 g) red pepper flakes, to taste

¼ teaspoon sea salt

¼ teaspoon black pepper

Remove the seeds from your cucumbers by slicing the cucumber in half lengthwise and scraping out the seeds using a spoon. Then dice the cucumbers and add them to a mixing bowl. Add the chiles and chopped cilantro.

In a small bowl, whisk together the vinegar, agave, lime juice, red pepper flakes, salt, and pepper. Add to the cucumber mixture and toss to coat. Keep refrigerated until ready to serve.

YIELD: 8 servings

ITALIAN GRILLED CORN AND WHITE BEAN SALAD

ITALY
USA

This is another one of those dishes that is great for omni potlucks: it's full of fresh veggies and great flavor, with no noticeable "weird" vegan ingredients (the nooch sneaks in here nicely!) to scare anyone off.

1 recipe Italian Grilled Corn (page 110), plus any reserved droppings from the rub

¼ cup (60 ml) olive oil

¼ cup (60 ml) red wine vinegar

1 tablespoon (10 g) minced garlic

1 tablespoon (11 g) Dijon mustard

3 cups (70 g) tightly packed baby or wild arugula

2 ½ cups (650 g) white beans, drained and rinsed

2 ounces (56 g) bulb fennel, thinly julienned

2 Roma tomatoes, seeded and diced

5 large leaves basil, chiffonade

Remove the kernels from the corn and place in a mixing bowl.

Whisk together the remaining spice rub, olive oil, vinegar, minced garlic, and mustard in a small bowl and set aside.

To the mixing bowl containing the corn, add the arugula, white beans, fennel, tomatoes, and basil. Add the dressing and toss to coat. Serve immediately, or chill until ready to serve. (Personally I like it a little warm, but my husband prefers it cold.)

YIELD: 8 side dish servings

CABBAGE AND NOODLE SALAD

CHINA
USA

This scrumptious salad gets a bitter bite from radicchio. Don't like radicchio? Use red cabbage (or more green cabbage) instead.

1 pound (454 g) dry chow mein (or spaghetti or linguine) noodles, cooked according to package directions, drained, and cooled

2 tablespoons (30 ml) vegetable oil

2 cups (140 g) finely shredded cabbage

2 cups (120 g) finely shredded radicchio

3 tablespoons (45 g) sesame oil

2 tablespoons (30 ml) soy sauce

2 tablespoons (16 g) black sesame seeds

While the noodles are cooking, prepare the cabbage mix. Heat the vegetable oil in a pan over medium-high heat. Add the cabbage and radicchio and sauté until reduced in size by half, about 2 minutes. Remove from the heat and set aside to cool.

Toss together the cabbage-radicchio mixture, cooled noodles, sesame oil, soy sauce, and sesame seeds. Serve cold.

YIELD: 8 servings

COCONUT CURRY PEA AND POTATO CHOWDER

- Gluten Free
- Soy Free
- Nut Free

INDIA
USA

This hearty soup is very easy to throw together, and then you can relax while it simmers and fills the house with the warm, savory smells of curry.

2 tablespoons (30 ml) olive oil

1 stalk leek, white and light green parts, thinly sliced

4 cups (940 ml) vegetable broth

1½ cups (353 ml) full-fat coconut milk

3 pounds (1.4 kg) russet potatoes, peeled and cubed

1½ cups (200 g) green peas

2 tablespoons (12 g) curry powder, store-bought or homemade (see tip)

salt and pepper to taste

In a soup pot with a tight-fitting lid, heat the oil over medium-high heat. Add the leeks and sauté until lightly browned and fragrant, about 2 to 3 minutes.

Add the broth, coconut milk, potatoes, peas, and curry powder, stir, and bring to a boil. Reduce to a simmer, cover, and simmer for 30 to 45 minutes, or until the potatoes are very tender. The longer you cook it, the thicker it becomes, because the potatoes break apart and release their starch.

Add salt and pepper to taste, then serve.

YIELD: About 10 cups (2.3 L)

FUSION TIP

Sure, it's easy to pick up a bottle of premade curry powder, but if you mix your own, you can adjust it to your own specific tastes! Just mix together 5 teaspoons ground coriander, 1 to 2 teaspoons chili powder, 1 to 2 teaspoons ground turmeric, 1 teaspoon ground cumin, 1 teaspoon five-spice powder, and ½ to 1 teaspoon black pepper; store in an airtight container in a cool, dry place. Yield: About ¼ cup (24 g)

SESAME CARROT COLESLAW

- Quick and Easy
- Soy Free
- Nut Free

CHINA
USA

This crunchy coleslaw is great as a side dish on its own, and also perfect to top all kinds of fusion dishes, from the Spicy Korean Barbecue Jackfruit (page 96) to the Teriyaki Seitan Asada Tacos (page 103).

1 cup (70 g) finely shredded cabbage

½ cup (54 g) finely shredded carrot

1 teaspoon black sesame seeds

¼ teaspoon red pepper flakes

1 tablespoon (15 ml) sesame oil

2 tablespoons (30 ml) rice vinegar

Toss together all the ingredients to coat, and refrigerate until ready to serve.

YIELD: 4 servings

YA KA MEIN (a.k.a. "Old Sober")

(see photo, page 74)

(see photo, page 74)

CHINA
KOREA
USA

So, I was watching the Food Network, and they had an episode of *Chopped* that featured Louisiana chefs as all four contestants. One of the contestants was known as the Ya-Ka-Mein Lady. (Her real name is Ms. Linda Green.)

What is ya ka mein? It is a beef-based broth with beef, spiced up with Cajun spices, poured over spaghetti noodles, and topped with scallion and a hard-boiled egg. I was fascinated by this dish. Asian-inspired Louisiana soul food? Well, if that isn't fusion, what is!?

There is some controversy over how the dish ended up in Louisiana. Some say it was the black soldiers fighting in Korea who brought it back to the States. Others say it was the Chinese workers brought over to work on the railroad between Houston and New Orleans, who eventually settled in the now defunct New Orleans Chinatown and popularized the dish. Regardless of how it got there, the locals revel in its ability to "cure" hangovers, hence the moniker "Old Sober."

I am going to give you two ways to make this, one super easy and semi-homemade, and one that is completely from scratch. Both are yummy, both make use of a funky fun tofu "deviled egg," and both taste great! I hope you enjoy it as much as I do.

1 pound (454 g) dry spaghetti noodles

6 ½ cups (1.5 L) ya ka mein broth, store-bought or homemade (recipe follows)

2 tablespoons (30 ml) soy sauce (only if using store-bought broth)

1 teaspoon Old Bay Seasoning

½ teaspoon smoked paprika

½ teaspoon dried oregano

¼ teaspoon cayenne pepper, or to taste (¼ teaspoon makes it pretty darn spicy!)

1 pound (454 g) prepared seitan, store-bought or homemade (recipe follows), cut into bite-size chunks

8 tofu deviled eggs (recipe follows, optional)

½ cup (25 g) chopped scallion

Prepare the pasta according to the package instructions.

While the pasta is boiling, add the broth to a separate pot along with the soy sauce, Old Bay, paprika, oregano, and cayenne pepper. Bring the broth to a boil, and reduce to a simmer. Add the seitan chunks, cover, and simmer for 20 minutes.

Divide pasta among 4 big bowls. Spoon one-fourth of the seitan and broth over the noodles. Place two deviled eggs on top of each bowl, sprinkle with the scallion, and serve.

For ya ka mein broth:

6 cups (1.4 L) water

½ cup (120 ml) soy sauce

¼ cup (60 ml) vegan Worcestershire sauce

2 tablespoons (16 g) garlic powder

2 tablespoons (16 g) onion powder

black pepper, to taste

Add all the ingredients to a pot, stir, and proceed with the recipe instructions above.

For seitan chunks:

1 cup (144 g) vital wheat gluten flour

1 teaspoon onion powder

1 teaspoon garlic powder

¼ teaspoon salt

¼ teaspoon black pepper

¾ cup (180 ml) water

1 tablespoon (15 ml) soy sauce

¼ cup (60 ml) vegetable oil

Add all the dry ingredients to a mixing bowl, and stir to combine. Add the water and soy sauce and knead until a very elastic and wet dough is formed. Allow to rest for 20 minutes.

Tear the dough into bite-size chunks.

Heat the oil in a frying pan over medium-high heat. Add the chunks to the hot oil, taking care not to overcrowd the pan. Fry for 2 to 3 minutes per side, or until dark golden brown and crispy. Transfer the fried chunks to the simmering broth for 20 minutes, return to the frying pan and fry to crisp, and then continue with the recipe instructions above.

For tofu deviled eggs:

1 block (12 to 16 ounces, or 340 to 454 g) extra-firm or super-firm tofu, drained and pressed

1 tablespoon (11 g) prepared yellow mustard

¼ cup (60 ml) extra-virgin olive oil

1 teaspoon mellow white or yellow miso

½ teaspoon garlic powder

½ teaspoon onion powder

½ teaspoon paprika, plus a pinch for finishing

½ teaspoon turmeric

salt and pepper, to taste (black salt will give it an extra eggy flavor)

Cut the block of tofu in half. Cut one half into 8 rectangular blocks about 2-inches long x 1¼ inches wide x ¾-inch tall (5 x 3.8 x 2 cm). Using a spoon, scoop out a little "bowl" in each block, then set aside.

Add the remaining half of the tofu block, the scooped-out tofu from the "bowls," and all the remaining ingredients to a blender or food processor and purée until very smooth. Roll the mixture into little balls and place inside the bowls you made in the tofu blocks. (Use any leftover mixture as a yummy sandwich spread, or just eat it all up with a spoon!) Sprinkle with a tiny pinch of paprika before placing on top of the ya ka mein.

YIELD: 4 big bowls

CREAMY CILANTRO PEPITA PESTO POTATO SALAD

This has a little kick, but it makes a great addition to any potluck. It also doesn't scream, "I'm vegan!" because it doesn't appear to contain any "weird" ingredients (the tofu is hidden in the sauce)!

2 ½ pounds (1.2 kg) red potatoes, skin on, cut into bite-size chunks

1 cup (160 g) finely diced red, white, or yellow onion

1 cup (101 g) chopped celery

1 cup (16 g) chopped fresh cilantro

1 cup (120 g) hulled pumpkin seeds

1 cup (235 ml) Creamy Cilantro Pepita Pesto Sauce (page 22)

1 cup (150 g) Sweet and Spicy Cilantro-Cucumber Salad (page 53)

salt and pepper to taste

Boil the potatoes in lightly salted water until fork-tender. Drain and cool completely. Add all the remaining ingredients and toss to mix thoroughly. Keep refrigerated until ready to serve.

YIELD: 8 servings

CHINESE-STYLE MACARONI SALAD

● Quick and Easy

CHINA
USA

This macaroni salad is versatile and makes great use of odds and ends in your fridge. As written it calls for carrots, green beans, celery, scallion, corn, sugar snap peas, and cashews. An equally great salad would use edamame, green peas, chopped broccoli or cauliflower, mandarin orange segments, and almond slivers or slices. What about jicama, lima beans, zucchini, purple cabbage, and cucumbers? Or how about adding the leftover bok choy stalks from the Sweet Chile Grilled Tofu and Bok Choy Sandwiches (page 103)? Basically, about 1 cup of any vegetable you have lying around plus macaroni plus dressing equals a fun new take on everyone's favorite potluck dish—macaroni salad!

1 pound (454 g) elbow macaroni, prepared according to package instructions

1 cup (108 g) shredded carrot

1 cup (250 g if using canned, 125 g if using frozen) yellow corn kernels

1 cup (120 g) diced celery

1 cup (114 g) fresh green beans, chopped into 1-inch (2.5 cm) pieces

1 cup (100 g) finely chopped scallion

1 cup (114 g) sugar snap peas, stems removed

1 cup (112 g) cashew pieces (raw or roasted is fine)

1 cup (235 ml) Sweet Chile Sauce (page 21)

2 tablespoons (16 g) black or white sesame seeds

Add the cooked and cooled macaroni to a large mixing bowl. Add all the other ingredients and toss to combine. Keep refrigerated until ready to serve.

YIELD: 8 servings

FUSION TIP

Add some chopped tofu, seitan, tempeh, or your favorite vegan protein substitute for a complete meal.

SWEET CHILE POTATO SALAD COLESLAW

THAILAND

USA

My dad begged me to add a "fusion" recipe that combined his love for mashed potatoes mixed with coleslaw. Umm, Dad, that's not exactly what fusion is. Whatever. This is for my dad.

2 pounds (908 g) red potatoes

1 cup (235 ml) Sweet Chile Sauce (page 21)

1 block (12 ounces, or 340 g) soft silken tofu

3 cups (210 g) finely shredded green cabbage

1 cup (160 g) finely diced yellow onion

1 cup (109 g) pecan halves

¼ cup (15 g) chopped fresh parsley

Cut the potatoes into small bite-size chunks and bring to boil in a large pot of water. Boil until fork-tender, drain, and return to the pot to cool.

While the potatoes are boiling, make the dressing. In a blender, whiz together the chile sauce and tofu until creamy and smooth. Set aside.

To the cooled potatoes, add the cabbage, onion, pecans, and parsley. Top with dressing and toss to combine. Keep refrigerated until ready to serve.

YIELD: 8 servings

INDIAN-SPICED BLACKENED TOFU GREEN SALAD

INDIA

USA

I would be remiss if I didn't include at least one green salad in a vegan cookbook, right? I suggest the Sesame-Garlic Ginger Miso Dressing (page 20), but the Creamy Cilantro Pepita Pesto Sauce (page 22) would also be a lovely flavor here—the perfect salad to serve up family style, or to pre-portion for easy lunches during the week.

For salad:

1 ½ cups (45 g) baby spinach, firmly packed

2 cups (180 g) shredded green cabbage, firmly packed

1 cup (20 g) wild or baby arugula, firmly packed

1 cup (110 g) shredded carrots, firmly packed

3 tablespoons (7.5 g) fresh basil chiffonade

½ cup (50 g) chopped scallion

½ cup (8 g) fresh chopped cilantro

1 cup (235 ml) Sesame Garlic Ginger Miso Dressing (page 20)

For blackened tofu:

¼ cup (60 ml) olive oil

1 tablespoon (7 g) nutritional yeast

1 teaspoon paprika

½ teaspoon each: garlic powder, onion powder, turmeric, and salt

¼ teaspoon each: ground cumin, ginger, coriander, and black pepper

⅛ teaspoon ground cinnamon

⅛ teaspoon ground cardamom

1 block (12 to 16 ounces, or 340 to 454 g) extra-firm or super-firm tofu, drained and pressed

¼ cup (16 g) hulled pumpkin seeds

¼ cup (40 g) raisins or dried cranberries

¼ cup (23 g) sliced almonds

To make the salad, toss together the spinach, cabbage, arugula, carrots, basil, scallion, and cilantro in a large bowl and set aside. If serving immediately, go ahead and toss in the dressing, or place the dressing on the table so that each person can dress his or her own salad.

To make the tofu, mix together the oil, nutritional yeast, and all of the spices in a small bowl to form a wet spice rub.

Cut the tofu into 16 finger-size pieces.

Heat a frying pan over medium heat.

Coat each piece of tofu with the spice rub and add to the frying pan. Panfry until the spices are blackened, rotating each piece until all sides have been cooked. Transfer to a plate.

Arrange the tofu on top of the dressed salad. Sprinkle the pumpkin seeds, cranberries, and almonds all over the top and serve.

YIELD: 4 main dish servings

BARLEY AND BROWN RICE TABBOULEH

This hearty (and healthy) version of tabbouleh is a snap to toss together, especially if you always keep cooked grains on hand … ha ha, yeah right! But seriously, you can cook the grains ahead of time, and when you are ready to make the salad, it's just a matter of a little chopping and a little tossing!

2 cups (320 g) prepared
   brown rice, chilled

1 cup (157 g) prepared barley, chilled

2 Roma tomatoes, seeded
   and finely diced

1 cup (60 g) finely chopped
   fresh parsley

½ cup (80 g) finely diced white onion

¼ cup (25 g) finely chopped scallion

2 tablespoons (12 g) finely
   chopped fresh mint

¼ teaspoon ground cinnamon

¼ cup (60 g) olive oil

3 tablespoons (45 ml) lemon juice

salt to taste

Toss all the ingredients together in a mixing bowl and chill before serving.

YIELD: 8 servings

FUSION TIP

Use this to add bulk to your wraps and pita sandwiches. It also tastes awesome piled on top of a leafy green salad.

SIMPLE MISO BROTH

○ Quick and Easy
○ Nut Free

JAPAN
USA

This broth couldn't be any easier, even if it came out of a package!

4 cups (940 ml) water

1 teaspoon finely ground kelp

3 tablespoons (48 g) white or yellow miso paste, or to taste

¼ cup (25 g) finely chopped scallion

Add the water and kelp to a pot. Bring to a boil over high heat, reduce to a simmer, and stir in the miso paste. Simmer until the miso paste dissolves completely, about 2 to 3 minutes. Stir in the scallion. Keep warm until ready to serve.

YIELD: 4 cups (940 ml)

SWEET CHILE TOFU NOODLE BOWL

○ Nut Free

THAILAND
JAPAN
USA

This noodle bowl tastes excellent hot or cold, which makes it perfect to prepare ahead of time for easy weekday lunches.

1 package (10 ounces, or 280 g) chow mein, udon, or ramen noodles

1 recipe Simple Miso Broth (see above)

1 bell pepper, diced

¼ cup (27 g) shredded carrot

1 recipe Sweet Chile Grilled Tofu (page 102)

¼ cup (4 g) chopped cilantro

Sweet Chile Sauce (page 21), optional

Prepare the noodles according to package instructions. Once cooked, drain and run under cool water. Distribute evenly among 4 bowls. Add 1 cup (235 ml) of the miso broth to each bowl. Top each bowl with some bell pepper, carrot, 3 tofu triangles, and cilantro. If you like it extra spicy, drizzle on additional chile sauce for extra kick. Serve.

YIELD: 4 servings

CHIMI CORN AND BLACK BEAN SALAD

This fresh salad gets an extra punch of good for you from the kale and quinoa. No feeling guilty about this one!

ARGENTINA

USA

4 ears Chimi Grilled Corn (page 110), kernels removed from the cobs

1 ½ cups (384 g) cooked or canned black beans

2 cups (370 g) prepared quinoa

1 bunch (3 cups, or 201 g) lacinto kale with stems removed, chopped

1 red bell pepper, seeded and diced

¼ cup (4 g) chopped fresh cilantro

2 tablespoons (30 ml) olive oil

2 tablespoons (30 ml) lime juice

1 teaspoon minced garlic

¼ teaspoon ground cumin

⅛ teaspoon cayenne pepper (optional)

salt and pepper to taste

Add the corn, beans, quinoa, kale, bell pepper, and cilantro to a mixing bowl.

In a separate bowl, mix together the olive oil, lime juice, garlic, cumin, cayenne pepper, salt, and pepper. Pour the dressing over the salad and toss to coat. Chill before serving.

YIELD: 8 side dish servings

GINGER-COCONUT CARROT BISQUE

● Quick and Easy
● Gluten Free
● Soy Free

This sweet and savory, creamy soup gets just a hint of sass from the addition of chopped fresh ginger.

THAILAND

USA

2 cups (470 ml) vegetable broth

1 can (14 ounces, or 392 ml) coconut milk

1 pound (454 g) carrots, peeled and sliced into coins

1 tablespoon (6 g) minced fresh ginger

1 tablespoon (10 g) minced garlic

salt and pepper to taste

Add all the ingredients to a pot and bring to a boil over high heat. Reduce to a simmer and simmer until the carrots are nice and tender, about 10 minutes. Using an immersion blender or a traditional blender, purée until smooth.

YIELD: 5 cups (1.2 L)

SWEET AND SPICY TOFU AND ARUGULA SALAD

● Quick and Easy

THAILAND
CHINA
USA

This creamy salad just screams with all sorts of flavors. Sweet, spicy, savory, crunchy, fruity, nutty, peppery... it has it all. I like this one just fine on its own, but wrap it up in a tortilla, now that is a tasty lunch!

1 pound (454 g) extra-firm tofu, drained and pressed, panfried if desired

3 ounces (84 g) wild arugula

¼ cup (35 g) raisins

¼ cup (32 g) chopped dried apricots

¼ cup (30 g) pine nuts

¼ cup (16 g) raw shelled pepitas (pumpkin seeds)

¼ cup (46 g) diced roasted red pepper

½ medium red onion, finely diced

½ cup (120 ml) Creamy Sesame Sriracha Sauce (page 16)

¼ cup (60 ml) Sweet Chile Sauce (page 21)

salt and pepper, to taste

Chop the tofu into small cubes and add to a large mixing bowl. Add the arugula, raisins, apricots, pine nuts, pumpkin seeds, roasted red pepper, and onion.

In a small bowl, whisk together the Creamy Sesame Sriracha Sauce, Sweet Chile Sauce, salt, and pepper. Add the dressing to the salad and toss to coat.

YIELD: 4 main dish or 8 side dish servings

FUSION TIP

Like it really spicy? Substitute chopped fresh jalapeños for the roasted red peppers.

FUSION RICE BOWL

MEXICO
JAPAN
INDIA

This is a complete meal in a bowl! And who doesn't love a bowl? The recipe makes enough for eight people, and it is really a great way to serve a big group. Make the rice, chop the veg, set up a station, and let everyone make their own bowls. It also packs well, so it is a perfect meal for lunches to go.

¼ cup (60 ml) vegetable oil

2 cups (360 g) uncooked jasmine rice

3 cups (705 ml) vegetable broth, divided

1 can (15 ounces, or 420 g) diced tomatoes with juices

1½ cups (360 g) chickpeas, drained and rinsed

1 cup (160 g) diced yellow onion

½ teaspoon curry powder, store-bought or homemade (page 55)

salt and pepper to taste

2 cups (60 g) fresh spinach, chiffonade

1 cup (110 g) shredded carrot

1 cup (235 ml) Creamy Sesame Sriracha Sauce (spicy, page 16), Sara's Peruvian Aji Sauce (medium, page 18), or Nori Garlic Ranch (mild, page 24)

1 cup (100 g) chopped scallion

⅓ cup (90 g) Cotija-Style Tofu Crumbles (page 112)

1 tablespoon (8 g) black and/or white sesame seeds

Heat the oil in a large frying pan over medium-high heat. Add the rice and toss to completely coat. Cook until the rice is toasted and lightly browned, about 5 minutes, stirring constantly. Stir in 2 cups (470 ml) of the vegetable broth, tomatoes, chickpeas, onion, curry powder, salt, and pepper. Bring to a simmer and continue to simmer until the rice has absorbed all the liquid and is tender, adding the remaining 1 cup (235 ml) broth as needed.

To assemble the bowls, start with the rice, then layer on the spinach and carrot. Drizzle liberally with the sauce, top with the scallions and tofu crumbles, then finish it off with a sprinkle of sesame seeds.

YIELD: 8 servings

INDIAN-SPICED PUMPKIN AND JACKFRUIT CHILI

This chili received some awesome feedback at my neighborhood chili cook-off. I made this without beans (true chili has no beans!), but I think the addition of beans or lentils could prove fantastic in this chili.

INDIA
USA

2 tablespoons (30 ml) olive oil

1 cup (160 g) finely diced onion

2 tablespoons (20 g) minced garlic

1 fresh jalapeño, finely diced

1 teaspoon chili powder

1 teaspoon garam masala

½ teaspoon ground coriander

½ teaspoon turmeric

½ teaspoon ground cumin

¼ teaspoon red pepper
    flakes, or to taste

1 can (20 ounces, or 566 g) jackfruit,
    packed in water or brine,
    rinsed and drained

1 cup (235 ml) all-natural
    root beer (not diet!)

1 can (15 ounces, or 425 g)
    crushed tomatoes

½ cup (122 g) pumpkin purée

salt and pepper to taste

nondairy sour cream, for
    serving (optional)

chopped cilantro, for
    serving (optional)

Heat the olive oil in a pot over medium-high heat. Add the onion and sauté for 2 to 3 minutes, until fragrant. Add the garlic and sauté an additional 2 to 3 minutes. Add the jalapeño, chili powder, garam masala, coriander, turmeric, and red pepper flakes. Stir to combine.

Add the jackfruit and toss to combine. Use the edge of your spoon or spatula to break up the jackfruit as it cooks. Continue to cook for an additional 2 minutes. Add the root beer, tomatoes, and pumpkin. Stir to combine. Reduce the heat to low, and continue to cook, constantly stirring, until the jackfruit is stringy and tender, about 10 minutes. Season with salt and pepper. Serve garnished with nondairy sour cream and chopped cilantro.

YIELD: 4 servings

FAUX PHO BROTH

○ Low Fat
○ Nut Free

VIETNAM
USA

I used to eat pho almost every day when I worked in Venice Beach. I went to a pho bar, where there were about thirty different veggies and other toppings so I could create my own bowl every time!

6 cups (1410 ml) low-sodium vegetable broth

⅓ cup (80 ml) soy sauce or tamari

¼ cup (40 g) diced white or yellow onion

1 tablespoon (6 g) minced fresh ginger

1 tablespoon (10 g) minced garlic

1 whole cinnamon stick

¼ teaspoon aniseed

Add all the ingredients to a pot, stir, and bring to a boil over high heat. Reduce to a simmer, and simmer for 30 minutes. Strain out the solids and keep hot over low heat until ready to serve.

YIELD: 6 cups (1.5 L)

SLOPPY JOE PHO

○ Low Fat

VIETNAM
USA

This is a pretty loose interpretation of a sloppy joe and of pho! But the end result is a savory soup that warms your insides! I call for rice vermicelli (a.k.a. rice sticks), but you can use any kind of noodles that you like. (P.S. I know it's pronounced *fuh*.)

2 tablespoons (30 ml) olive oil

1 medium bell pepper (any color), seeded and diced

1 cup (160 g) diced white or yellow onion

1 teaspoon minced garlic

2 tablespoons (34 g) ketchup

½ teaspoon smoked paprika

¼ teaspoon black pepper

1 recipe Faux Pho Broth (above), divided

¾ cup (72 g) dry TVP granules or finely chopped seitan

1 package (10 ounces, or 280 g) rice vermicelli noodles, prepared

¼ cup (25 g) chopped scallion, for garnish

¼ cup (4 g) chopped cilantro, for garnish

1 fresh jalapeño, sliced, for garnish (optional)

Sriracha sauce (optional)

In a sauté pan, heat the oil over medium heat. Add the bell pepper, onion, and garlic. Sauté until fragrant and the onions are translucent, about 5 minutes. Stir in the ketchup, paprika, and black pepper. Add 1 cup (235 ml) of the prepared broth. Stir in the TVP. Remove from the heat, cover, and let stand for 10 minutes.

To assemble the soup, divide the noodles evenly among 4 large soup bowls. Top with a generous helping of the Sloppy Joe mixture. Add one-fourth of the remaining broth. Garnish with the scallion, cilantro, and jalapeño. Squirt in a smidge of Sriracha, and serve.

YIELD: 4 main dish servings

CHAPTER 4

THE TWISTED TABLE
MAIN DISHES

Ahh, yes! On to the main course. The star of the plate. The main event. On the following pages you will find recipes that are sure to tickle the senses with a fusion of flavor from all over the world!

GARLIC-ORANGE SEITAN BITES

USA
CHINA

These sweet little nuggets of protein goodness are awesome over rice and vegetables, and make for a great addition to salads, and for a little extra fusion goodness, as a filling for tacos and burritos!

1 cup (144 g) vital wheat gluten flour

1 teaspoon onion powder

1 teaspoon garlic powder

1 tablespoon (1 g) freeze-dried chives

½ teaspoon black sesame seeds

¾ cup (180 ml) water

1 tablespoon (15 ml) soy sauce

4 cups (940 ml) chicken-flavored vegetable broth

vegetable oil, for frying

2 cups (470 ml) Garlic Orange Sauce (page 19)

Add the flour, onion powder, garlic powder, chives, and sesame seeds to a mixing bowl, and stir to combine. Add the water and soy sauce and knead until a very elastic and wet dough is formed. Allow to rest for 20 minutes.

Bring the vegetable broth to a simmer in a pot over medium heat. Tear the dough into about 40 bite-size chunks.

Heat enough oil to coat the bottom of a frying pan over medium-high heat. Add the chunks to the hot oil, taking care not to overcrowd the pan. Fry for 2 to 3 minutes per side, or until dark golden brown and crispy. Transfer the fried chunks to the simmering broth and simmer for 20 minutes.

Transfer back to the frying pan and fry again until crisped. Add the Garlic Orange Sauce to the frying pan and toss to coat. Heat until warmed through.

YIELD: About 40 pieces

KOFTA KEBABS

● Nut Free

USA
PAKISTAN

Kofta kebabs are a Middle Eastern "meatloaf" on a stick. They are a popular street food, and make for great appetizers. You can serve them on the stick with dipping sauce, or slide them into a roll (hot-dog style) to make a delicious sandwich, adding your favorite fixin's.

1 cup (96 g) dry TVP granules

2 teaspoons (12 g) sea salt

2 tablespoons (16 g) dried minced onion

1 tablespoon (2 g) dried parsley

1 tablespoon (7 g) ground coriander

1 teaspoon ground cumin

½ teaspoon ground cinnamon

½ teaspoon ground allspice

¼ teaspoon cayenne pepper

¼ teaspoon ground ginger

¼ teaspoon ground black pepper

1 cup (235 ml) boiling water

1⅔ cups (240 g) vital wheat gluten flour

1 tablespoon (8 g) cornstarch

¼ cup (60 ml) canola or other mild-flavored vegetable oil, plus more for brushing

¼ cup (60 ml) vegan Worcestershire sauce

¼ cup (60 ml) water

1 tablespoon (10 g) minced garlic

8 buns (optional), for serving

Mix together the TVP granules and all of the dry spices in a heat-proof bowl. Pour in the boiling water and stir to combine. Cover and let stand for 10 minutes. Allow to cool enough to handle. Add the gluten and cornstarch and mix to coat.

In a separate small bowl, mix together the ¼ cup (60 ml) oil, Worcestershire sauce, water, and minced garlic. Add to the TVP mixture and mix until well incorporated. Cover and allow to rest for 20 to 30 minutes. From here you can make your mixture into kebabs or burgers.

To make kebabs, make sure you have soaked your skewers in water for at least 20 minutes. Divide the mixture into 8 equal portions. Form around the skewer, into a hot dog shape, leaving at least 3 to 4 inches (7.5 to 10 cm) at the non-pointy end. These kebabs cook up best on the grill (or in a grill pan). Be sure to brush each kebab with additional oil before placing on the grill. This will help prevent sticking, add more flavor, and ensure you get the best grill marks. Place on a medium-hot spot on the grill and cook for 5 to 6 minutes per side. You can serve the kebabs alone or on a bun, hot dog style.

To make burgers, form them into patties and grill or bake them in a single layer, uncovered, on a baking sheet at 350°F (180°C, or gas mark 4) for a total of 40 minutes, flipping halfway through. Serve with your favorite sauce for dipping; my favorite is Creamy Sesame Sriracha Sauce (page 16).

YIELD: 8 kebabs or burgers

TAMALE SHEPHERD'S PIE

MEXICO
USA

This is one of those recipes that takes a few hours to make, but it makes a big casserole, so you'll have enough for dinner and also for lunches throughout the week. You can also make these in individual ramekins, and pipe the topping on with a giant star tip, making for a wonderful presentation. Just reduce the cooking time accordingly.

For sweet potato topping:

3 pounds (1362 g) sweet potatoes, peeled and cubed

1 cup (235 ml) full-fat coconut milk

2 tablespoons (30 ml) coconut oil, melted

1 tablespoon (6 g) curry powder

¼ teaspoon chipotle powder

salt and pepper to taste

For tamale crust:

3 cups (360 g) instant masa flour (I use Maseca brand)

1 tablespoon (7 g) paprika

1 teaspoon garlic powder

1 teaspoon onion powder

½ teaspoon coriander

½ teaspoon salt

¼ teaspoon black pepper

1 fresh jalapeño, seeded, cored, and finely diced

1 cup (235 ml) vegetable oil

1½ cups (355 ml) water

For coconut curry filling:

2 tablespoons (30 ml) coconut oil

1 medium yellow onion, diced (about 2 cups)

2 large portobello caps, diced

1 cup (134 g) green peas

1 cup (108 g) shredded carrot

1 can (15 ounces, or 420 g) chickpeas, drained and rinsed

2 teaspoons curry powder

½ cup (120 ml) full-fat coconut milk

Have ready a 9 x 12-inch (23 x 30.5 cm) casserole dish.

To make the topping, add the sweet potatoes to a pot and add enough water to cover. Bring to a boil, reduce and simmer until fork-tender. Drain and return to the pot. Add the coconut milk, coconut oil, curry powder, chipotle powder, salt, and pepper. Using an electric mixer, beat until fluffy and very few lumps remain. Set aside.

To make the tamale crust, add the masa flour, paprika, garlic powder, onion powder, coriander, salt, pepper, and diced jalapeño to a mixing bowl and stir to combine. Add the oil and water and knead to mix. The resulting masa should be wet but firm. Press the masa evenly into the bottom of the casserole, and set aside.

Preheat the oven to 350°F (180°C, or gas mark 4).

To make the coconut curry filling, heat the coconut oil over medium-high heat. Add the onion and mushrooms, and sauté for 5 to 7 minutes, or until reduced by half. Stir in the peas, carrot, and chickpeas. Mix the curry powder into the coconut milk, and stir into the pot. Continue to cook for 2 more minutes. Remove from the heat and spread the filling evenly over the masa crust. Evenly spread the sweet potato topping over the filling.

Bake for 45 minutes to 1 hour, until the masa is firm but still moist and the curry filling is slightly browned on top. Remove from the oven, and allow to rest for 10 minutes before cutting and serving.

YIELD: 12 servings

CRUNCHY THAI FLATBREAD PIZZA

I love salads on top of pizza, and this one is no exception. The contrast of warm, soft, saucy bread and crunchy, cool veggies is a wonderful culinary treat for the senses.

For crust:

2 tablespoons (18 g) cornmeal

2 cups (240 g) all-purpose flour

1 cup (120 g) whole wheat flour

1 teaspoon dried basil

1 teaspoon garlic powder

½ teaspoon sea salt

½ teaspoon baking powder

½ teaspoon baking soda

¼ teaspoon red pepper flakes

1¼ cups (295 ml) water

olive oil, for brushing

For salad:

1 cup (235 ml) Thai Peanut
   Sauce (page 21), divided

3 cups (210 g) shredded cabbage
   (a mix of green and red is nice)

¼ cup (28 g) cashews

1 can (15 ounces, or 420 g)
   mandarin oranges, drained

¼ cup (22 g) finely sliced fennel bulb

1 teaspoon black sesame seeds

To make the crust, preheat the oven to 350°F (180°C, or gas mark 4). Dust a baking sheet with the cornmeal.

In a large mixing bowl, mix together the flours, basil, garlic powder, salt, baking powder, baking soda, and red pepper flakes. Slowly add the water and knead until a nice dough ball is formed. Continue to knead for about 2 minutes.

Dust a flat surface with flour and begin to flatten it out to your desired shape and thickness. I usually shape it to fit the cookie sheet. Brush the edges with olive oil. Spread ½ cup (120 ml) of the Thai Peanut Sauce all over the surface of the pizza.

Bake for 20 to 25 minutes, until the edges begin to lift from the pan and the crust is beginning to brown.

While the pizza crust is baking, toss together the cabbage, cashews, mandarin oranges, fennel, and sesame seeds.

Once the crust has baked, remove from the oven and pile the cabbage mixture evenly on top. Drizzle with the remaining ½ cup (120 ml) Thai Peanut Sauce. Slice and serve.

YIELD: 8 slices

SESAME MEATLOAF WITH SPICED KETCHUP

INDIA | This hearty meatloaf tastes great with some Spicy Roasted Broccoli (page 120) and a heaping
USA | pile of Wasabi Mashed Potatoes (page 123). Use leftovers to make a killer meatloaf sandwich
on thick grilled French bread with and a big schmear of Creamy Sesame Sriracha Sauce
(page 16).

2 ½ cups (588 ml) vegetable
  broth or water

2 tablespoons (30 ml) soy sauce

3 cups (288 g) dry TVP granules

1 ½ cups (150 g) finely diced
  scallion, divided

1 tablespoon (10 g) minced garlic

2 tablespoons (30 ml) sesame oil

1 tablespoon (8 g) black
  sesame seeds, divided

1 teaspoon ground black pepper

1 cup (235 ml) Spiced Ketchup
  (page 23), plus more for
  basting and drizzling

1 ½ cups (216 g) vital
  wheat gluten flour

Bring the vegetable broth and soy sauce to a boil
in a pot over medium-high heat. Stir in the TVP,
remove from the heat, cover, and let stand for at
least 10 minutes to absorb the liquid.

Add 1¼ cups (125 g) of the scallion, garlic, sesame
oil, 2 teaspoons of the sesame seeds, pepper,
Spiced Ketchup, and vital wheat gluten flour to
the reconstituted TVP. Mix well. Use your hands to
knead the mixture together. Take half of the mixture and place it in a food processor and process
until it is the consistency of paste.

Mix the two portions back together with your hands.
The point of this step is to get your meatloaf to stick
together better when you slice it. Allow it to rest for
at least 20 minutes, and up to overnight.

Preheat the oven to 350°F (180°C, or gas mark 4).
Oil a 9 x 5-inch (23 x 12.5 cm) loaf pan.

Press the mixture into the prepared loaf pan very
tightly. Pack it in as tightly as you can. Seriously.
Push hard. Harder.

Bake for 20 minutes. Remove from the oven and
brush a thin layer of ketchup on the top. Return to
the oven and bake an additional 25 minutes.

Remove from the oven, let stand for 10 minutes,
and then turn out onto a serving dish. Garnish with
¼ cup (25 g) scallion and the remaining 1 teaspoon
sesame seeds. And of course, serve with a big
drizzle of extra Spiced Ketchup (page 23)!

YIELD: 8 servings

INTERNATIONAL FAIR OF TAMALES

I know it may seem counterintuitive, but whenever I see a bunch of leftovers starting to pile up in my fridge or freezer, I think to myself, "Time to make tamales!" And when I make tamales, I usually make at least one full batch of forty. So here's the deal. I have found that so many of the dishes throughout this book make excellent fillings for tamales. Use a good base masa and a variety of fun fillings for fusion tamales that are sure to excite and satisfy those taste buds, especially when served up with a variety of sauces. Plus, they freeze so well. So spend an afternoon with your friends and family making up a batch of tamales, and then have a bunch of easy-go-to meals ready for you in the freezer!

40 cornhusks

For masa:
8 cups (960 g) masa harina

2 tablespoons (14 g) paprika

2 tablespoons (36 g) salt

1 tablespoon (7 g) ground cumin

2 tablespoons (16 g) chili powder

3 tablespoons (24 g) garlic powder

2 cups (470 ml) corn or vegetable oil

2 quarts (2 L) vegetable broth, warm (not hot)

Some of my favorite fillings:
Hot, Sweet, and Sour Seitan Ribs (without the Lemongrass Bones) (page 88)

Spicy Korean Barbecue Jackfruit (page 96)

Chimi Grilled Corn (page 110)

Smoky Chili-Lime Sweet Potatoes (page 118)

Soak your husks in warm water for at least 2 hours.

To prepare the masa, place the masa flour in a large mixing bowl. Add the dry spices to the flour and mix until completely incorporated. Add the oil to the masa and spice mixture. Slowly add the broth 1 cup (235 ml) at a time. Knead the mixture with your hands to form a dough with the consistency of peanut butter. If it is too thin, add more masa; if it is too thick, add more broth or warm water.

Remove the husks from the water and carefully separate them. Stack them on a kitchen towel where they will be easy to access. Spread about ¼ cup (70 g) of the masa onto the husk from the center all the way to one edge of the husk. Leave enough space to roll up and fold over the pointy end. Add about 2 tablespoons (about 30 g) of filling to the center of the masa. Starting at the edge with the masa, roll up the tamale, then fold over the pointy end. If desired, tie a strip of husk around the tamale.

Pack the tamales in a steamer basket tightly so they are standing upright, open side up, and won't fall over. Place enough water in the bottom of the pot so that it does not touch the tamales. Bring it to a boil, and then reduce the heat to medium-low and steam for 2 to 3 hours. Remember to check on the water level every once in a while so that the

(continued on page 84)

pot does not boil dry. After 2 hours of steaming, remove one tamale, and place it on a plate to cool for 5 minutes. Unwrap it and test for doneness. It should be its own "unit" and not mushy or runny.

If it is done, awesome! If not, continue to steam for another 15 to 30 minutes, and repeat the test. Place on a tray to cool, or place in resealable bags to freeze. You can freeze tamales for up to a year. (But mine never last that long.)

To reheat, I usually just heat them up in the microwave for about 2 minutes, wrapped in a paper towel, but if you are antimicrowave, try thawing them in the refrigerator overnight and then heating them, either in a steamer for about 15 minutes, or, like they do in Mexico, on a griddle: heat a griddle to fairly hot, put the tamales (still in the cornhusk wrappers) on the griddle, and toast until the cornhusks are nearly black on all sides. Peel and eat.

YIELD: 40 tamales

FUSION TIP

Need tamales in a hurry? Try using a pressure cooker. Thanks to the fine folks at HipPressureCooking.com and tester extraordinaire Kelly, who worked out the timing for this recipe, you can have your tamales cooked in 20 minutes versus 2 hours! Follow the recipe as directed above, but instead of packing your tamales into the steamer, add 2 cups (470 ml) of water and a steamer basket to the bottom of your pressure cooker. Add the tamales, standing upright and closely packed, and lock the pressure cooker lid. Turn the heat up to high and when it reaches pressure, lower the heat to maintain pressure. Cook for 20 minutes, at high pressure, then remove the pressure cooker from the heat and wait for the pressure to come down on its own, about 10 minutes (otherwise known as the natural release method). Test for doneness. If not done, relock the cover, bring back to pressure, and cook an additional 5 minutes at high pressure. Again, let the pressure come down on its own.

BEAN BALL BAHN MI (see photo, page 74)

USA
CHINA
VIETNAM

This really is a fun sandwich, full of all sorts of crazy flavors that really go together well.

1 small baguette (8 inches, or 20 cm) crusty French bread

2 tablespoons (30 ml) Creamy Sesame Sriracha Sauce (page 16)

5 Hot, Sweet, and Sour Bean Balls (below), warmed

¼ cup (36 g) California Curtido Kimchi (page 107)

Slice open the baguette and slather each side with 1 tablespoon (15 ml) of the sauce. Place the bean balls in a single row. Top with the kimchi. Enjoy!

YIELD: 1 sandwich

HOT, SWEET, AND SOUR BEAN BALLS

● Nut Free

USA
CHINA

These little balls have a nice bite to the outside, but are soft and chewy on the inside. They taste awesome in the Bean Ball Bahn Mi (above).

3 cups (375 g) white beans, drained and rinsed

1 teaspoon garlic powder

1 teaspoon onion powder

3 tablespoons (45 ml) soy sauce

1 cup (144 g) vital wheat gluten flour

½ cup (50 g) finely chopped scallion

¼ cup (60 ml) vegetable oil

1 cup (235 ml) Hot, Sweet, and Sour Sauce (page 23)

Preheat the oven to 350°F (180°C, or gas mark 4). Line a baking sheet with parchment paper.

Add the beans, garlic powder, onion powder, and soy sauce to a food processor and process until a crumbly dough forms. Add the gluten and combine.

Transfer the dough to a mixing bowl. Knead in the scallion, and form a ball of dough. Allow to rest for 20 minutes so the gluten can develop. Roll about 1 tablespoon (22 g) of dough into a ball and place on the baking sheet. Repeat until all the dough is used. You should get about thirty balls.

Bake for 30 minutes, flipping the balls halfway through. Remove from the oven.

Heat the oil in a frying pan over medium-high heat. Sauté the balls in the hot oil until a crispy crust forms, about 2 minutes, turning constantly. Carefully add the sauce and toss to coat.

YIELD: About 30 pieces

WONTON WRAPPER LASAGNA NAPOLEONS

CHINA
ITALY

Oooh, so pretty! If you ever really want to impress your friends with your plating skills and creative culinary talents, pull this one out of your back pocket! (They never have to know how easy it is.)

32 vegan wonton or pot sticker wrappers, thawed

¼ cup (60 ml) olive oil, divided

1 cup (235 ml) Spiced Ketchup (page 23), divided

3 Roma tomatoes, seeded and finely diced

2 cups (360 g) Cotija-Style Tofu Crumbles (page 112)

1 cup (48 g) fresh basil chiffonade

¼ cup (34 g) capers, drained

¼ cup (34 g) chopped black or kalamata olives

salt and pepper to taste

Preheat the oven to 350°F (180°C, or gas mark 4). Line 2 baking sheets with parchment paper or a baking mat.

Bring a large pot of lightly salted water to a boil over medium-high heat. Carefully add the thawed wonton wrappers, one at a time, to the boiling water. Take care not to overcrowd the pot. Cook until al dente, remove from the pot, lay in a single layer on the baking sheets, and brush very lightly with oil.

Place a thin layer of ketchup on all of the wrappers, using about ½ cup (120 ml). Sprinkle a small amount of the diced tomatoes and tofu crumbles on each of the wrappers. Bake for 20 minutes, or until the wrappers are firm.

While they are baking, warm the remaining ½ cup (120 ml) ketchup.

On a serving plate, carefully stack 8 (for tall) or 4 (for short) wrappers directly on top of one another. Drizzle the top with the remaining warmed ketchup. Top with fresh basil chiffonade, capers, olives, and a final drizzle of olive oil. Add salt and fresh cracked pepper to taste. Serve immediately.

YIELD: 4 tall or 8 short napoleons

CABBAGE-FETTUCCINE ALFREDO

USA
ITALY

This dish aims to prove that pasta isn't really necessary to have a rich and hearty pasta dinner. Shredded green cabbage stands in for the noodles and a creamy cashew sauce makes for the Alfredo.

2 tablespoons (30 ml) olive oil

1 tablespoon (15 g) minced garlic

1 shallot, finely diced

6 cups (420 g) shredded green cabbage

salt and pepper to taste

2 tablespoons (30 ml) lemon juice

2 cups (470 ml) full-fat coconut milk

½ cup (60 g) nutritional yeast

½ cup (56 g) raw cashews, ground into a fine powder

1 tablespoon (16 g) tahini

2 tablespoons (36 g) mellow white or yellow miso

2 tablespoons (16 g) cornstarch

1 tablespoon (8 g) onion powder

1 tablespoon (8 g) garlic powder

1 tablespoon (6 g) ground mustard powder

Heat the oil in a large pot over medium-high heat. Add the garlic and shallot and sauté until fragrant, about 2 to 3 minutes. Add the cabbage and a pinch of salt. Toss and continue to cook until the cabbage is wilted and translucent and reduced in size by about half, about 5 minutes. Stir in the lemon juice and set aside.

To make the sauce place the coconut milk, nutritional yeast, ground cashews, tahini, miso, cornstarch, onion powder, garlic powder, and mustard powder into a blender and blend until very smooth. Pour into a sauce pot and heat over medium heat, stirring constantly, until it thickens, about 5 to 7 minutes. Pour over the cooked cabbage and toss to coat. Season with salt and pepper to taste.

YIELD: 4 large servings

HOT, SWEET, AND SOUR SEITAN RIBS WITH LEMONGRASS BONES

● Nut Free

USA

CHINA

The lemongrass used for the "bones" gives a nice, citrusy aroma to the seitan, besides looking like the real thing. It's a long list of ingredients, but it comes together pretty easily.

3 cups (432 g) vital wheat gluten flour

½ cup (60 g) whole wheat pastry flour

¼ cup (30 g) nutritional yeast

¼ teaspoon red pepper flakes

¼ teaspoon salt

1 cup (160 g) diced yellow onion

½ cup (50 g) diced scallion

1 tablespoon (10 g) minced garlic

2 cups (470 ml) Hot, Sweet, and Sour Sauce (page 25), divided

1 cup (235 ml) water

¼ cup (60 ml) soy sauce or tamari

2 tablespoons (30 ml) olive oil

2 tablespoons (34 g) ketchup

2 tablespoons (30 ml) sesame oil

1 tablespoon (15 g) Chinese hot mustard or Dijon mustard

1 teaspoon Sriracha

½ teaspoon liquid smoke

5 stalks lemongrass, outer layers removed, cut into 4 equal pieces (20 total)

In a large bowl, combine the flour, whole wheat pastry flour, nutritional yeast, red pepper flakes, salt, onion, scallion, and garlic. In a separate bowl whisk together 1 cup (235 ml) of the Hot, Sweet, and Sour Sauce, water, soy sauce, olive oil, ketchup, sesame oil, hot mustard, Sriracha, and liquid smoke.

Add the wet mixture to the dry and combine. Knead until an elastic dough is formed. Some of the onions will fall out—set aside. Let the dough rest for 20 minutes.

Divide the dough into 4 equal pieces. Flatten the pieces into a rectangular shape and place on a baking sheet lined with parchment paper or a baking mat. The dough is still very elastic, making this fairly difficult, but that's normal. Allow to rest for an additional 20 minutes.

Preheat the oven to 350°F (180°C, or gas mark 4).

Once again, form the dough into rectangles. Push 5 stalks of the lemongrass through each piece of dough, about 1 inch (2.5 cm) apart. Repeat until all 4 pieces each have 5 "bones." Brush each "rack" of ribs generously with the remaining 1 cup (235 ml) Hot, Sweet, and Sour Sauce on both sides. Sprinkle the reserved onions on top of the ribs. Cover the pan loosely with foil, to create a steam tent. Bake for 1 hour.

After 1 hour, remove from the oven, flip, brush on another thick layer of sauce, and return to the oven for 30 more minutes, uncovered. Remove from the oven and brush on a final layer of sauce before serving. Discard the lemongrass bones.

YIELD: 4 racks of ribs

SESAME-SRIRACHA SEITAN CRUMBLES

● Quick and Easy
● Nut Free

USA
JAPAN

This method was developed by Celine Steen (you may remember her Seitan Chorizo Crumbles from *500 Vegan Recipes*). You can use these in the Spicy Seitan Pot Stickers (page 43), tacos, tamales, burritos, or anywhere a spicy, meaty crumble would be tasty.

½ cup (72 g) vital wheat gluten flour

½ teaspoon smoked paprika

½ teaspoon onion powder

¼ teaspoon chipotle powder

¼ teaspoon salt

⅛ teaspoon black pepper

¼ cup (60 ml) water

1 tablespoon (15 ml) Sriracha sauce

1 tablespoon (15 ml) soy sauce

2 teaspoons sesame oil

1 tablespoon (15 ml) vegetable oil, for sautéing

Add the flour and spices to a large mixing bowl and mix well.

In a separate bowl, combine the water, Sriracha, soy sauce, and sesame oil. Add the wet mixture to the dry and combine using your fingertips. Break the dough apart into little crumbles.

Heat the vegetable oil in a frying pan over medium-high heat. Add the crumbles to the pan and sauté for 3 to 4 minutes, or until browned and dry.

YIELD: Just over 1 cup (150 g)

THAI PEANUT CHICKEN AND WAFFLES

USA
THAILAND

Combining savory waffles with spicy fried "chicken" and drizzled with creamy Thai peanut sauce makes for a fantastic take on tradition. Serve on a bed of greens, if desired.

For waffles:

1 cup (235 ml) unsweetened almond or soy milk

2 tablespoons (30 ml) lemon juice

¼ cup (60 ml) warm water

2 tablespoons (13 g) ground flaxseed

2 tablespoons (30 ml) vegetable oil

2 cups (240 g) all-purpose flour or whole wheat pastry flour

2 teaspoons baking powder

1 teaspoon freeze-dried chives, or 1 tablespoon (1 g) fresh

½ teaspoon sea salt

½ teaspoon paprika

½ teaspoon garlic powder

¼ teaspoon freshly ground black pepper

To make the waffles, preheat your waffle iron. Mix together the milk and lemon juice and set aside to curdle and thicken.

In a small bowl, whisk together the warm water and ground flaxseed. Add the vegetable oil and stir to combine.

In a separate mixing bowl, mix together the flour, baking powder, chives, salt, paprika, garlic powder, and pepper.

Add the oil and flax mixture to the milk mixture and mix well. Add the wet mixture to the dry and stir to combine; do not overmix.

Add the mixture to your waffle iron and cook six waffles according to manufacturer's instructions.

For chicken:

1 pound (454 g) extra-firm or super-firm tofu, drained and pressed

1 cup (235 ml) vegetable broth

¼ cup (60 ml) soy sauce

2 tablespoons (30 ml) sesame oil

2 cups (240 g) all-purpose flour or whole wheat pastry flour

½ teaspoon cayenne pepper

¼ teaspoon paprika

¼ teaspoon garlic powder

¼ teaspoon onion powder

¼ teaspoon freshly ground black pepper

1 cup (235 ml) unsweetened almond, soy, or coconut milk

1 tablespoon (15 ml) Sriracha sauce

Vegetable oil, for frying

To make the chicken, cut the tofu into 12 finger-size pieces.

In a shallow dish, mix together the vegetable broth, soy sauce, and sesame oil. Place the tofu fingers in the dish and gently toss to coat in the mixture. Allow to rest in the marinade for at least 1 hour and up to overnight.

In a flat dish or wide bowl, mix together the flour and all of the spices.

In a separate bowl, combine the milk and Sriracha.

In a heavy-bottomed skillet or frying pan, pour the vegetable oil to a depth of ¼ inch (6 mm). Heat over medium-high heat until a tiny bit of the flour mixture dropped into the oil sizzles.

Lightly coat each piece of the marinated tofu in the flour mixture, then dip into the coconut milk, and then dredge one last time in the flour mixture. Get a nice thick flour coating on each piece. Place each piece into the pan and fry until golden and crispy, about 1 full minute, then flip and repeat on the other side. I do mine in two batches, waiting a minute or two in between to let the oil reheat. Remove from the pan, and place on a plate lined with paper towels to absorb any excess oil.

1 recipe Thai Peanut Sauce (page 21)

2 limes, cut into 6 wedges each

chopped scallion, for garnish (optional)

red pepper flakes, for garnish (optional)

To assemble, place two fried tofu fingers on each waffle and drizzle liberally with the Thai Peanut Sauce. Serve with lime wedges to squirt over the top. Garnish with scallion and red pepper flakes.

YIELD: 6 servings

FUSION TIP

The waffles freeze quite well. Separate each waffle with a sheet of parchment or waxed paper and then place inside a freezer bag.

MISO MAC AND CHEESE

JAPAN
USA

I sure love me some mac and cheese, and this one doesn't disappoint. A little bit of sass from the peppers and a little bit of crunch from the panko really satisfy my cravings for a warm, hearty, curl-up-on-the-couch-with-a-bowl of mac and cheese! I really like to top mine with a healthy dollop of Spiced Ketchup (page 23), a habit I picked up from my mom growing up, when she used to top the boxed variety of macaroni and cheese with a big old squirt of tomato ketchup.

1 pound (454 g) dry pasta, prepared according to package instructions

1 recipe Miso Mustard Cheese Sauce (page 26), divided

1 cup (80 g) panko bread crumbs, divided

2 whole roasted bell peppers, seeded and diced (I love roasted jalapeños, but for the not-so-spicy, roasted red peppers add great flavor!)

2 tablespoons (30 ml) olive oil

Preheat the oven to 400°F (200°C, or gas mark 6).

In a large bowl, add the pasta, most of the sauce—reserving 1/2 cup (120 ml) for later use—1/2 cup (40 g) of the panko, and the diced peppers and stir to combine. Add the mixture to an ovenproof casserole and top with the remaining 1/2 cup (120 ml) sauce. Sprinkle the remaining 1/2 cup (40 g) panko over the top. Drizzle the olive oil evenly over the top.

Bake for 25 minutes, or until the panko is golden.

YIELD: 8 side dish or 4 main dish servings

PUPUSAS GORDA

● Nut Free

EL SALVADOR
USA

From deep within El Salvador, the people of the Pipil tribe invented pupusas centuries ago. It wasn't until the late 1900s that a civil war in that country caused the people of El Salvador to migrate, sharing this national treasure with the rest of the Americas. Traditional pupusas are similar to a thick corn tortilla filled with any number of fillings. My version is a bit fatter than a traditional pupusa, almost as thick as a Mexican gordita (hence the name). I also added a lot of flavor to the dough itself. These can be served on their own, dipped into your favorite sauce, or even used as the base for all sorts of toppings, including coleslaws and green salads. Enjoy!

For dough:

2 ½ cups (300 g) masa harina

¼ cup (4 g) chopped fresh cilantro

1 teaspoon smoked paprika

1 teaspoon salt

½ teaspoon ground cumin

½ teaspoon garlic powder

½ teaspoon onion powder

½ teaspoon dried oregano

1 ½ cups (355 g) vegetable broth

2 tablespoons (30 ml) vegetable oil

2 tablespoons (30 ml) lime juice

For filling:

½ cup (90 g) Cotija-Style Tofu Crumbles (page 112)

¼ cup (125 g) prepared black beans

1 red or green jalapeño, seeded and finely diced

Vegetable oil, for frying

To make the pupusa dough, in a mixing bowl, combine the masa harina, cilantro, paprika, salt, cumin, garlic powder, onion powder, and oregano.

In a separate bowl, combine the vegetable broth, oil, and lime juice. Add the wet mixture to the dry and knead for 2 to 3 minutes, until a stiff dough forms. Divide the dough into 8 equal portions. Flatten each portion into patties about 4 inches (10 cm) in diameter.

To make the filling, in a small bowl, mix together the tofu crumbles, black beans, and jalapeño.

Place one quarter (60 g) of the mixture in the center of 4 of the patties. Place the remaining 4 patties on top and seal the edges by pressing them together and rounding them out.

Pour oil to a depth of ½ inch (1.3 cm) into a pot and heat to 350°F (180°C) on a deep-frying thermometer. (I use a pot, so that I don't splatter oil all over the place.) Add the pupusas to the hot oil, being careful not to overcrowd the pan (you may need to do this in 2 batches) and fry each side until golden brown and crispy, about 2 minutes per side. Transfer to a plate lined with paper towels to absorb excess oil. Serve hot.

YIELD: 4 pupusas

SPICY KOREAN BARBECUE JACKFRUIT

○ **Nut Free** | Use this spicy meaty fruit in sandwiches, tacos, or burritos.

USA
KOREA

2 tablespoons (30 ml) vegetable oil

1 cup (160 g) diced onion

1 tablespoon (10 g) minced garlic

1 can (20 ounces, or 560 g) jackfruit in water or brine (NOT SYRUP!), drained and rinsed

1 cup (235 ml) cola made with real sugar

1 cup (235 ml) Spicy Korean Barbecue Sauce (page 26)

1 tablespoon (15 g) sambal oelek

salt to taste

In a skillet or pot with a tight-fitting lid, heat the oil over medium-high heat. Add the diced onion and sauté for 2 to 3 minutes, until fragrant and translucent. Add the garlic and continue to cook for 2 to 3 more minutes. Add the jackfruit and, using the edge of your spoon, begin to break it up as it cooks for 2 to 3 more minutes. Add the cola, barbecue sauce, and sambal oelek. Stir to combine and bring to a boil.

Reduce to a simmer, cover, and cook for 35 to 45 minutes, returning often to stir and prevent scorching. The sugars from the cola and barbecue sauce will caramelize and stick to the bottom of the pan if you aren't careful.

Cook until tender and most of the liquid is absorbed. The jackfruit should be tender and stringy. If needed, you can pull it apart with a fork. Add salt to taste.

YIELD: 4 to 6 servings

SPICY KOREAN BARBECUE JACKFRUIT BURRITOS

○ **Nut Free** | These filling burritos are bursting with fusion flavors and textures.

KOREA
MEXICO

1 recipe Cilantro Lime Rice with Toasted Coconut (page 106)

1 recipe Sesame Carrot Coleslaw (page 55)

1 cup (250 g) prepared black beans

1 recipe Spicy Korean Barbecue Jackfruit (above)

¼ cup (25 g) finely chopped scallion

4 burrito-size (10 inches, or 25 cm) tortillas, warmed

Layer all the ingredients in the center of a warm tortilla and roll up tightly.

YIELD: 4 big burritos

FRITTATA FOO YOUNG WITH ASPARAGUS-MUSHROOM GRAVY

USA
CHINA
ITALY

Egg foo young is a traditional Chinese egg pancake with vegetables and is usually served with a savory brown gravy. This version takes that idea and bakes it up like an Italian frittata!

For frittata:

24 spears asparagus

¼ cup (28 g) chopped sun-dried tomato

½ cup (80 g) diced red bell pepper

¼ cup (25 g) chopped scallion

2 cups (140 g) finely shredded cabbage, packed

1 block (12 ounces, or 340 g) soft silken tofu

1 block (12 ounces, or 340 g) extra-firm tofu, drained and pressed

¼ cup (30 g) nutritional yeast

2 tablespoons (30 ml) soy sauce

2 tablespoons (30 ml) olive oil

2 tablespoons (16 g) cornstarch

1 tablespoon (15 g) Dijon mustard

1 teaspoon onion powder

½ teaspoon each: dried parsley, thyme, and turmeric

⅛ teaspoon black salt

For asparagus-mushroom gravy:

2 tablespoons (30 ml) olive oil

1 shallot, thinly sliced

1 tablespoon (10 g) minced garlic

24 remaining asparagus stems, broken into 2-inch (5 cm) pieces, tough ends discarded

1 ounce (28 g) dried shiitake mushrooms

1½ cups (355 ml) water

2 tablespoons (30 ml) soy sauce

1 tablespoon (18 g) mellow white or yellow miso paste

1 tablespoon (8 g) nutritional yeast

Preheat the oven to 400°F (200°C, or gas mark 6). Have ready a well-oiled 10-inch (25 cm) cast-iron skillet or greased baking dish.

To make the frittata, trim the tips of the asparagus, and set the stems aside. Chop the tips into 3 pieces and add to a bowl with the sun-dried tomato, bell pepper, scallion, and cabbage.

Add tofus, nutritional yeast, soy sauce, oil, cornstarch, mustard, and spices to a blender and purée. Pour the mixture over the vegetables and toss to coat. Pour into the prepared skillet and spread evenly.

Bake 50 to 60 minutes, or until browned and firm, and the edges pull away from the sides of the pan.

To make the gravy, heat the oil over medium-high heat. Add the shallot and garlic and sauté about 2 to 3 minutes. Add the asparagus stems, toss to coat, and cook an additional 2 minutes, while tossing. Pour the sautéed mixture carefully into a blender. Add the mushrooms, water, soy sauce, miso, and nutritional yeast and purée. Return mixture to the pan and heat to keep warm.

Once the frittata is baked, remove from the oven, and cool for 15 minutes. Once set, invert onto a serving plate. Top with the asparagus-mushroom gravy, or serve on the side.

YIELD: 6 servings

TERIYAKI SEITAN ASADA STRIPS

These delicious strips of juicy, flavorful pineapple teriyaki seitan serve up great over rice or steamed veggies. I also love them in tacos! (See page 103.)

JAPAN
MEXICO

¾ cup (108 g) vital wheat gluten flour

¼ cup (30 g) whole wheat pastry flour

½ teaspoon paprika

½ teaspoon garlic powder

½ teaspoon onion powder

⅓ cup (80 ml) water

2 tablespoons (30 ml) soy sauce

1 tablespoon (15 ml) vegan Worcestershire sauce

½ teaspoon liquid smoke

1 cup (235 ml) Pineapple Teriyaki Sauce (page 25)

2 to 3 tablespoons (30 to 45 ml) vegetable oil, for sautéing

chopped scallion, for garnish (optional)

sesame seeds, for garnish (optional)

Add the vital wheat gluten, whole wheat pastry flour, paprika, garlic powder, and onion powder to a mixing bowl and stir to combine.

In a separate bowl, mix together the water, soy sauce, Worcestershire, and liquid smoke. Add the wet mixture to the dry and knead for 2 to 3 minutes until a very elastic dough is formed. Cover and let rest for 30 minutes.

Preheat the oven to 350°F (180°C, or gas mark 4).

Shape the dough into a log and place in the center of a piece of foil or parchment paper, roll up, and twist the ends tightly to close. Place the log on a baking sheet, seam side down, and bake for 1 hour, flipping halfway through. Remove from the oven and allow to cool enough to handle.

Once cooled, slice into thin strips about 1-inch wide x 4½-inches long (2.5 x 11.5 cm). These measurements are just a reference; they need not be exact.

Add the Pineapple Teriyaki Sauce to a pot and heat over medium-low heat.

Heat 1 tablespoon (15 ml) of the vegetable oil in a frying pan over medium-high heat. Add the seitan strips in a single layer and panfry for 2 to 3 minutes, or until dark golden brown and crispy. Flip and repeat on the other side. Once both sides are crispy, transfer immediately to the pot of teriyaki sauce. Repeat with the remaining 1 to 2 tablespoons (15 to 30 ml) oil and seitan strips until all of the pieces have been added to the sauce. Toss the seitan to coat, and keep warm until ready to serve.

Serve garnished with scallions and sesame seeds.

YIELD: 4 main dish servings

SWEET CHILE GRILLED TOFU

CHINA

USA

This tofu is super easy to make, plus it works well on its own as a main dish, over rice, or on top of a salad. It is especially tasty in the Sweet Chile Grilled Tofu and Bok Choy Sandwiches (opposite).

1 block (16 to 20 ounces, or 454 to 570 g) extra-firm or super-firm tofu, drained and pressed

1 cup (235 ml) Sweet Chile Sauce (page 21)

½ cup (120 ml) rice wine

chopped fresh cilantro, for garnish

Cut the block of tofu into 12 triangles. I do this by first cutting the tofu into 3 equal pieces, then cut each of those 3 pieces into 4 equal triangles.

Place the tofu and Sweet Chile Sauce in a shallow dish and marinate in the refrigerator for at least 4 hours and up to overnight. Make sure all of the tofu is coated in sauce. After marinating, remove the tofu, and reserve the leftover sauce for use later in this recipe.

Cook the tofu either in a grill pan over medium-high heat or on a grill over a medium flame for about 4 to 5 minutes per side, ensuring you get those sought-after grill marks. The sugar in the marinade will aid in the process by getting dark and caramelized. Remove from the grill and transfer to a serving dish.

Add the reserved marinade and rice wine to a small saucepan. Bring to a boil and boil for about 1 minute, stirring constantly, to ensure all of the sugar is completely dissolved. Pour the sauce over the grilled tofu. Garnish with the fresh cilantro and serve.

YIELD: 4 servings

SWEET CHILE GRILLED TOFU AND BOK CHOY SANDWICHES

● Nut Free

CHINA

USA

This sandwich tastes awesome on grilled sourdough, but really steals the show when served bahn mi style in a crusty baguette, topped with the California Curtido Kimchi (page 107).

1 large bunch bok choy, stems removed

2 tablespoons (30 ml) olive oil

salt and pepper to taste

¼ cup (60 ml) Creamy Sesame Sriracha Sauce (page 16)

8 slices sourdough bread, toasted or grilled, or 4 crusty baguettes

1 recipe Sweet Chile Grilled Tofu (opposite)

Heat 1 tablespoon (15 ml) of the olive oil in a grill pan or frying pan over medium-high heat. Add half of the bok choy in a single layer and cook for about 2 minutes per side, until bright green and wilted and just a bit browned. Sprinkle with salt and pepper to taste as you are cooking. Repeat with the remaining 1 tablespoon (15 ml) oil and the remaining half of the bok choy.

Spread 1 tablespoon (15 ml) of sauce on each slice of bread. Distribute the bok choy evenly onto four of the slices. Add three triangles of tofu on top of each. Top with the remaining slices of bread and enjoy!

YIELD: 4 sandwiches

TERIYAKI SEITAN ASADA TACOS

JAPAN

MEXICO

The sweet, juicy asada combined with the almost bitter crunch of the coleslaw topped with the creamy heat of the sauce makes these tacos a real fiesta in your mouth.

16 small (6 inches, or 15 cm) corn tortillas

1 recipe Teriyaki Seitan Asada Strips (page 100)

1 recipe Sesame Carrot Coleslaw (page 55)

½ cup (120 ml) Creamy Sesame Sriracha Sauce (page 16), for drizzling

½ cup (50 g) finely chopped scallion

½ cup (30 g) chopped fresh cilantro

Heat a dry pan over medium-high heat and warm the tortillas until lightly browned on each side. Stack two tortillas for each taco. You will make eight total tacos. Layer the ingredients as follows: three strips of teriyaki seitan, about ½ cup (54 g) of coleslaw, a generous drizzle of sauce, and a sprinkling of scallion and cilantro.

YIELD: 8 tacos

CHAPTER 5

NIBBLE AND NOSH
SIDES AND SNACKS

No meal would be complete without a supporting cast. This chapter is filled with a mix of flavors from all over the world twisted and contorted together into some amazing new dishes!

CILANTRO LIME RICE WITH TOASTED COCONUT

● Gluten Free
● Soy Free

This flavorful rice makes a great addition to any meal as a side dish, or as an excellent filling for the Spicy Korean Barbecue Jackfruit Burritos (page 96).

MEXICO
THAILAND

2 tablespoons (30 ml) vegetable oil

1 cup (180 g) dry basmati rice

1¾ cups (415 ml) water

¼ cup (60 ml) lime juice

1 teaspoon minced garlic

½ teaspoon ground cumin

½ cup (8 g) chopped fresh cilantro

¼ cup (30 g) unsweetened coconut flakes, toasted (see tip)

salt and pepper to taste

In a large skillet with a tight-fitting lid, heat the oil over medium heat. Add the dry rice and toss to coat. Continue to cook until the rice is toasted and beginning to brown. This process can take up to 10 minutes. Carefully add the water and stir. Add the lime juice, garlic, and cumin. Stir to combine and bring to a boil. Reduce to a simmer, cover, and simmer until tender and the liquid has been absorbed, about 10 minutes. Stir often to prevent the rice from sticking to the bottom of the pan. Stir in the cilantro, toasted coconut, salt, and pepper.

YIELD: 4 to 6 servings

FUSION TIP

To toast coconut, add flakes to a dry pan heated over medium-high heat. Toss frequently to prevent burning, and toast until lightly browned, about 2 minutes.

CALIFORNIA CURTIDO KIMCHI

● Low Fat

USA
EL SALVADOR
KOREA

This is truly a fusion of two countries' version of a very similar dish: Salvadoran curtido coleslaw and Korean kimchi. I will be the first to admit that I am not a huge fan of kimchi. The smell is usually enough to send me packing, but if you are like me, don't be afraid of this! These salty veggies are more pickled than fermented, and they taste amazing piled on sandwiches for extra crunch and flavor. This also tastes great as a side to heavy mains, such as pupusas (page 95). I love to make a huge batch and have it on hand for a few weeks' worth of uses, but feel free to cut back on the recipe if you only want a little bit.

3 ¼ cups (228 g) shredded red cabbage (about ¼ of average-size head)

3 ¼ cups (228 g) shredded green cabbage (about ¼ of average-size head)

4 small bunches baby bok choy, chopped

8 to 10 cloves garlic, thinly sliced (if you have huge cloves use 8, smaller cloves use 10)

2 fresh jalapeños, sliced into rounds

2 cups (216 g) shredded carrot

½ cup (8 g) chopped fresh cilantro

1 cup (100 g) chopped scallion

1 cup (101 g) chopped celery

1 cucumber, sliced into rounds

4 cups (940 ml) water

2 tablespoons (36 g) sea salt

¼ cup (60 ml) white vinegar

1 tablespoon (2 g) dried dill or 3 tablespoons (6 g) fresh

2 tablespoons (14 g) paprika

In a large heat-proof mixing bowl, toss together all of the chopped vegetables.

Bring the water and salt to a boil in a pot over medium-high heat, until all of the salt is fully dissolved. Pour the boiling salt water directly over the vegetables and toss to wilt. Add the vinegar, dill, and paprika, and toss to coat. Transfer to a container and place in the refrigerator for at least 4 hours. This gets better the longer it sits.

The vegetables keep for up to 2 weeks (probably longer than that) in an airtight container in the refrigerator. When serving, strain out the liquid.

YIELD: About 10 cups (1080 g)

AJI POTATO SAMOSAS

INDIA

PERU

I love, love, love samosas. I would eat them every day if I could. These are a little bit more Peruvian in flavor than traditional Indian potato samosa, and the result is awesome.

1 pound (454 g) red potatoes

½ cup (120 ml) Sara's Peruvian Aji Sauce (page 18)

½ cup (8 g) chopped fresh cilantro

½ cup (125 g) prepared black beans

¼ cup (30 g) pine nuts

1½ cups (45 g) baby spinach leaves

12 flour tortillas (10 inches, or 25 cm)

oil, for baking or frying

salt, pepper, and paprika for sprinkling (optional)

Cut the potatoes into bite-size chunks, skin on. Add to a pot of water and boil until fork-tender. Drain and return to the pot. Add the aji sauce, cilantro, black beans, pine nuts, and spinach. Stir to combine, making sure the potatoes are crumbled—broken up a bit, so all the ingredients are incorporated fully.

Warm the tortillas so that they are soft and pliable. Place a tortilla on a flat surface and cut off ½ inch (1.3 cm) of the rounded edges. Cut the remaining piece in half to make two long strips with rounded tops and bottoms. Start at the bottom of one strip, fold up the bottom corner to the opposite flat edge, and repeat two more times until you get to the top of the strip, making sure you leave a ½-inch (1.3 cm) tab to tuck and seal. Open it up into a cone. Place about 2 tablespoons (about 28 g) of filling in the center of the cone, and tuck in the tab to seal.

Cook as desired. These can be baked or fried: If baking, preheat the oven to 400°F (200°C, or gas mark 6). Line a baking sheet with parchment paper or a silicone baking mat. Lay the samosas on the baking sheet in a single layer and brush both sides liberally with oil. Sprinkle the tops with salt, pepper, and paprika. Bake for 15 minutes, or until crisp.

If frying, pour enough oil into the pan to a depth of ¼ inch (6 mm) and heat to 350°F (180°C). Carefully add samosas to the oil, and fry until crispy and golden, about 15 seconds per side. Transfer to a plate lined with paper towels, and sprinkle the tops with salt, pepper, and paprika.

YIELD: 24 samosas

CHIMI GRILLED CORN (see photo, page 104)

Quick and Easy | This flavorful grilled corn on the cob is super easy to make.

USA
ARGENTINA

4 ears corn on the cob, husks removed
⅓ cup (80 ml) Chimi Sauce (page 20)

Rub each ear of corn with the sauce, making sure to get it into all the nooks and crannies. Grill over medium-high heat until slightly browned but still firm, 10 to 15 minutes.

YIELD: 4 servings

ITALIAN GRILLED CORN

Quick and Easy
Nut Free | This sure is a snazzy way to serve up plain old corn on the cobb!

USA
ITALY

¼ cup (32 g) nutritional yeast
1 tablespoon (2 g) dried oregano
1 tablespoon (8 g) garlic powder
¼ teaspoon red pepper flakes
¼ teaspoon salt
¼ teaspoon black pepper
¼ teaspoon dried basil
¼ teaspoon dried thyme
2 tablespoons (30 ml) olive oil
4 ears corn on the cob, husks removed

In a small bowl, mix together the nutritional yeast, oregano, garlic powder, red pepper flakes, salt, pepper, basil, and thyme. This will be the spice rub for the corn.

Rub ½ tablespoon (8 ml) olive oil on each ear of corn so that the spice rub will stick. Over a plate, or in a large bowl, rub the spice mixture all over the corn, trying to get as much as possible to stick to the corn and pressing it in between the kernels. Lots will fall off, and that's okay; reserve it for use in the Italian Grilled Corn and White Bean Salad (page 54).

Preheat your grill or grill pan to medium-high and place the corn on the grill. Grill until slightly blackened on each side, about 5 minutes per side.

YIELD: 4 servings

ESQUITES

Nut Free

MEXICO
JAPAN
USA

Esquites are a popular Mexican street food. This snack is traditionally served in paper cups lined with mayonnaise. The corn is sautéed in butter and onions and the whole thing is topped with even more mayo, chile powder, lime juice, cheese, and sometimes sour cream. That's a bit dairy laden and heavy for me. This is my version, and a pretty loose interpretation of the original at that. Instead of mayo, I use Creamy Sesame Sriracha Sauce, but the Creamy Cilantro Pepita Pesto Sauce (page 22) would also taste wonderful here.

¼ cup (60 ml) olive oil

1 medium yellow onion, finely diced

2 tablespoons (20 g) minced garlic

1 fresh red jalapeño or ½ bell pepper, seeded and finely diced

1 teaspoon ground epazote

½ teaspoon dried safflower

4 cups (656 g) corn kernels

2 tablespoons (30 ml) lime juice

salt and pepper to taste

½ cup (120 ml) Creamy Sesame Sriracha Sauce (page 16), divided

½ cup (85 g) Cotija-Style Tofu Crumbles (above)

¼ cup (25 g) finely chopped scallion

¼ cup (4 g) chopped fresh cilantro

Heat the olive oil in a large frying pan over medium-high heat. Add the onion, garlic, jalapeño, epazote, and safflower. Sauté until fragrant and translucent, about 2 to 3 minutes. Add the corn kernels and continue to cook until the corn is bright yellow and cooked all the way through, about 3 to 4 minutes, stirring often. Stir in the lime juice, and remove from the heat. Season with salt and pepper.

Line each of 4 small bowls with 1 tablespoon (15 ml) of the sauce. Divide the sautéed corn evenly among the bowls. Top with the tofu crumbles. Drizzle on the remaining ¼ cup (60 ml) sauce, and garnish with the scallion and cilantro.

YIELD: 4 servings

COTIJA-STYLE TOFU CRUMBLES

● Nut Free

MEXICO

USA

Traditional cotija is a bland, salty, crumbly Mexican cheese similar in texture to feta. It is most often used as a topping for soups, salads, enchiladas, and tacos.

1 block (12 ounces, or 340 g) extra-firm or super-firm tofu, drained and pressed

½ teaspoon salt

½ teaspoon garlic powder

½ teaspoon onion powder

½ teaspoon dried oregano

¼ teaspoon ground cumin

¼ teaspoon chipotle powder

1 tablespoon (15 ml) rice vinegar

In a mixing bowl, using your fingers, crumble the tofu until it resembles crumbled feta. Mix in the spices and vinegar until well incorporated. Allow to sit overnight before using, to allow the tofu to absorb the flavors.

YIELD: 2 cups (340 g)

FUSION TIP

To make your crumbles even more dry and crumbly, after you press your tofu, freeze it. Thaw and press again to remove any remaining moisture, and then crumble until it resembles feta. The process of freezing tofu changes the texture completely. It also gives the tofu a yellowish color.

FRIED AND SMASHED CASSAVA MASALA

Nut Free

PERU
INDIA

Cassava is a starchy root vegetable available at most supermarkets. When searching it out you may find it under different names, including yuca, manioc, mogo, balinghoy, and tapioca root (yep, that's where tapioca starch comes from). When buying it fresh, it is long (12 to 18 inches, or 30 to 45 cm) and about 2 to 3 inches (5 to 7.5 cm) in diameter. It has a thick, rough, brown leathery skin that needs to be peeled before use. It can also be found in the frozen foods section of most Asian markets, where it has already been peeled and trimmed. Either can be used for this recipe.

1 pound (454 g) cassava, peeled and trimmed

¼ cup (60 ml) vegetable oil

1½ cups (355 ml) full-fat coconut milk

¼ teaspoon Sriracha sauce

¼ teaspoon red pepper flakes

⅛ teaspoon each ground coriander, ground cumin, ground cardamom, ground cloves, ground nutmeg, cinnamon, and black pepper

salt to taste

Chop the cassava into bite-size chunks.

Heat the oil in a pot over medium heat. Carefully add the cassava and fry for 5 to 7 minutes, or until lightly browned and tender. Remove from the heat.

In a small bowl, whisk together the coconut milk, Sriracha, red pepper flakes, coriander, cumin, cardamom, cloves, nutmeg, cinnamon, and pepper and add to the pot. Using a hand masher, smash the mixture together until it resembles lumpy mashed potatoes. I sometimes use my immersion blender to do this. Add salt to taste.

Yield: 4 servings

FUSION TIP

For a lower fat version, you can boil or steam the cassava chunks instead of frying them. Also, if you just can't find cassava, guess what? You can use potatoes!

MUSHROOM COUSCOUS

● Soy Free
● Nut Free

This super-simple side dish gets its flavor from dried mushrooms. Call me crazy, but I really think this tastes like what I remember "Oriental Flavor Top Ramen" tasted like.

EGYPT
JAPAN

1 tablespoon (15 ml) vegetable oil

2 shallots, thinly sliced

1 tablespoon (10 g) minced garlic

2 ounces (56 g) dried shiitake
  mushrooms, chopped

5 cups (1175 ml) water

2 cups (350 g) pearl couscous
  (a.k.a. Israeli couscous)

1 cup (134 g) green peas

1 red bell pepper, seeded and diced

salt and pepper to taste

Heat the oil in a pot over medium-high heat. Add the shallot and garlic and sauté until fragrant, about 2 minutes. Add the dried mushrooms and toss to coat. Carefully add the water and bring to a boil. Reduce to a simmer, and simmer for 5 minutes.

Stir in the couscous and simmer for 5 to 6 minutes, or until tender and most of the liquid has been absorbed. Stir in the peas and bell pepper and continue to cook until heated through. Add salt and pepper to taste, and serve.

YIELD: 8 side dish servings

NOT-CHOWS

● **Nut Free**

CHINA
MEXICO

Not only are these Chinese-influenced nachos a delicious way to get your snack on, but they also pack in a huge amount of veggies! This recipe yields two big plates, so feel free to cut it in half if you are noshing solo.

1 cup (250 g) black beans, drained and rinsed

½ cup (82 g) yellow corn

½ cup (67 g) green peas

½ cup (54 g) shredded carrot

½ cup (36 g) finely chopped broccoli florets

½ cup (80 g) diced red bell pepper

¼ cup (25 g) chopped scallion

¼ cup (4 g) chopped fresh cilantro

1 fresh jalapeño, cored and seeded

2 tablespoons (30 ml) lime juice

2 tablespoons (30 ml) soy sauce

1 teaspoon minced garlic

8 ounces (226 g) tortilla chips

2 cups (470 ml) Miso Mustard Cheese Sauce (page 26), warmed

In a mixing bowl, toss together the beans, corn, peas, carrot, broccoli, pepper, scallion, cilantro, jalapeño, lime juice, soy sauce, and garlic and set aside.

Place a layer of chips on each of 2 plates, followed by a layer of the bean mixture, and then a layer of cheese sauce. Repeat until all the ingredients are used.

YIELD: 2 servings

SESAME KALE CHIPS

INDIA
USA

Kale chips are all the rage right now. And at $5 (or more) per 2-ounce (56 g) bag, it can get to be a pretty pricy habit! Making them at home is so easy that there is really no reason not to indulge. This recipe is a great base (like a plain potato chip) that tastes pretty darn good. But, from here you can go crazy with flavors. Like it spicy? Add some chipotle powder to the mix. Like it smoky? Add a bit of liquid smoke. So many varieties can be had when you just add some of your favorite flavors.

5 cups (340 g) curly kale, chopped
  into chip-size pieces
½ cup (128 g) sesame tahini
¼ cup (60 ml) lemon juice
¼ cup (30 g) nutritional yeast
⅓ cup (80 ml) soy sauce

Preheat the oven at the lowest setting, or prepare your dehydrator for use.

Line 4 baking sheets (if using an oven) with parchment paper or a nonstick baking mat. Add the cut kale to a large mixing bowl.

In a separate bowl, mix together the tahini, lemon juice, nutritional yeast, and soy sauce. The mixture should be the consistency of a milkshake. If your tahini is very thick, you may need to add a little water.

Pour the tahini mixture over the cut kale, and toss to coat evenly. Arrange the coated kale in a single layer on the baking sheets. Bake for 1 hour (or follow the instructions on your dehydrator). Remove from the oven and flip. Bake for an additional 30 minutes, or until crisp. Allow to cool completely before packaging.

Store in a sealed container in a cool, dry place.

YIELD: 6 ounces (168 g)

SMOKY CHILI-LIME SWEET POTATOES

I love the contrast of sweet, smoky, spicy, and sour all in one bite in this super-easy dish. The hardest part is peeling the potatoes! These potatoes also make great fillings for tacos, burritos, and tamales.

MEXICO
USA

2 pounds (908 g) sweet potatoes, peeled and cubed

2 tablespoons (30 ml) coconut oil, melted

2 tablespoons (30 ml) lime juice

1 tablespoon (8 g) chili powder (as mild or hot as you like it!)

1 teaspoon garlic powder

½ teaspoon salt

½ teaspoon liquid smoke

Preheat the oven to 375°F (190°C, or gas mark 5). Have ready a baking sheet lined with parchment paper or a nonstick mat.

Place the sweet potatoes in a mixing bowl. In a separate small bowl, whisk together the oil, lime juice, chili powder, garlic powder, salt, and liquid smoke. Pour the mixture over the potatoes and toss to coat. Spread on the baking sheet in a single layer.

Bake for 30 minutes, remove from the oven and toss, return to the oven, and bake for an additional 30 minutes, or until the potatoes are tender and the edges are browned.

YIELD: 6 servings

TAHINI GARLIC-ROASTED CAULIFLOWER

Another super-simple side dish that adds tons of flavor to veggies!

USA
INDIA

½ cup (128 g) tahini

¼ cup (60 ml) soy sauce

1 tablespoon (10 g) minced garlic

2 tablespoons (15 g) nutritional yeast

1 teaspoon dried parsley

½ teaspoon paprika

¼ teaspoon black pepper

1 head (about 1½ pounds, or 680 g) fresh cauliflower, trimmed

¼ cup (25 g) chopped scallion

1 teaspoon white or black sesame seeds

Preheat the oven to 375°F (190°C, or gas mark 5). Line a baking sheet with parchment paper or a baking mat.

In a mixing bowl, whisk together the tahini, soy sauce, garlic, nutritional yeast, dried parsley, paprika, and black pepper. Add the cauliflower, and toss to coat. Arrange in a single layer on the baking sheet.

Bake for 25 to 35 minutes, or until tender yet still firm (cooked through but not mushy). Remove from the oven and transfer to a serving dish. Garnish with the scallion and sesame seeds.

YIELD: 4 servings

SPICY ROASTED BROCCOLI ➤

This broccoli is packed with flavor and cooks up super quick.

USA
THAILAND

¼ cup (60 ml) olive oil

8 to 10 cloves garlic, thinly sliced

1 pound (454 g) broccoli florets

2 tablespoons (30 ml) sesame oil

½ teaspoon sea salt

½ teaspoon red pepper flakes

Preheat the oven to 375°F (190°C, or gas mark 5). Line a baking sheet with parchment paper or a baking mat.

Heat the olive oil in a pan over medium-high heat. Add the garlic and fry until crispy and brown (like making garlic chips).

Place the broccoli in a bowl. Pour the hot olive oil and garlic onto the broccoli. Add the sesame oil, salt, and red pepper flakes. Toss to mix. Spread in a single layer on the prepared baking sheet and roast for 10 minutes, or until the broccoli is tender yet still firm (cooked through but not mushy).

YIELD: 4 servings

HOT, SWEET, AND SOUR CABBAGE

○ Quick and Easy
○ Low Fat
○ Nut Free

USA
CHINA

This version of fried cabbage is a tasty Chinese twist on a traditional Southern side. If you have the sauce ready beforehand, this tangy dish comes together in mere minutes!

¼ cup (60 ml) vegetable broth

4 cups (280 g) shredded green cabbage

½ cup (120 ml) Hot, Sweet, and Sour Sauce (page 25)

In a large frying pan or pot, heat the vegetable broth over medium-high heat. Add the cabbage and cook for 5 to 7 minutes, until tender and reduced in size by half. Pour in the sauce and toss to coat.

YIELD: 4 servings

WASABI GRILLED ASPARAGUS

○ Soy Free
○ Gluten Free
○ Nut Free
○ Quick and Easy

JAPAN
GREECE

This simple preparation makes for deliciously flavorful asparagus. If you want to be extra fancy, garnish with a pinch of lemon zest before serving.

1 teaspoon wasabi powder

2 tablespoons (30 ml) lemon juice

2 tablespoons (30 ml) olive oil

1 bunch asparagus, rough ends trimmed

Mix together the wasabi powder, lemon juice, and olive oil in a mixing bowl. Add the asparagus and toss to coat. Grill, either in a grill pan over medium-high heat or on a grill over a medium flame. Cook for about 3 minutes, rotate, and cook an additional 3 minutes.

YIELD: 4 servings

CILANTRO LIME CHILE CARROT COINS

○ Quick and Easy

MEXICO
USA

This method will pretty much work on any chopped vegetable, but the sweetness of the carrots really pairs nicely with the sauce.

2 pounds (908 g) carrots, peeled and sliced into coins

½ cup (120 ml) Cilantro Lime Chile Sauce (page 17)

Add the carrots to a pot of lightly salted water and bring to a boil over medium-high heat. Boil until fork-tender, about 5 to 7 minutes. Drain and return to the pot. Alternatively, you can steam the carrots for about 10 minutes, until tender. Add the sauce and toss to coat.

YIELD: 4 to 6 servings

WASABI MASHED POTATOES

○ Gluten Free
○ Soy Free
○ Nut Free

JAPAN
USA

These mashed potatoes are just subtly kissed with wasabi. Too much, and they wouldn't be as creamy and yummers like mashed potatoes are supposed to be... you know, the way they make you want to fill up a big old bowl and plop down on the couch with 'em?

5 pounds (2270 g) red potatoes, skin on, cut into bite-size chunks

6 ounces (170 g) silken tofu

½ cup (120 ml) full-fat coconut milk or almond milk

¼ cup (60 ml) sesame oil

1 tablespoon (6 g) wasabi powder

½ cup (50 g) chopped scallion

salt to taste

black sesame seeds, for garnish (optional)

Place the potatoes in a large pot filled with lightly salted water and bring to a boil over medium-high heat. Boil until the potatoes are soft and fork-tender.

While the potatoes are boiling, place the tofu, coconut milk, sesame oil, and wasabi powder in a blender and blend until smooth.

Once the potatoes are tender, drain and return to the pot. Pour the blended mixture on the potatoes and mash using a hand masher. Some lumps are okay. Fold in the scallion and add salt to taste. Serve garnished with a pinch of black sesame seeds.

YIELD: 8 servings

◄ GARLIC ORANGE BRUSSELS SPROUTS

○ Quick and Easy
○ Nut Free

Don't like brussels sprouts? Please try these ones. Adding a touch of Chinese take-out flavor to these itty-bitty cabbages might just make you a believer.

CHINA
USA

2 tablespoons (30 ml) olive oil

1 shallot, thinly sliced

1 pound (454 g) fresh brussels sprouts, cut in half

1 cup (235 ml) Garlic Orange Sauce (page 19)

In a large frying pan, heat the olive oil over medium heat. Add the shallot and brussels sprouts, cut side down, in a single layer and sauté for about 5 minutes, until fragrant and tender and the edges of the sprouts begin to brown. Flip and cook another 5 minutes. Add the sauce and toss to coat.

YIELD: 4 servings

GINGER SESAME STEAMED KALE

○ Quick and Easy
○ Gluten Free
○ Soy Free
○ Nut Free

Is there seriously anything kale can't do? I love it boiled, roasted, dehydrated, raw, whole, chopped and, in this case, steamed!

JAPAN
USA

2 bunches curly kale, stemmed and chopped into bite-size pieces

¼ cup (60 ml) orange juice

1 tablespoon (6 g) minced ginger

2 tablespoons (32 g) tahini

salt to taste

1 teaspoon sesame seeds

Bring a pot of water to a boil over medium-high heat. Add the kale to a steamer basket and steam for 10 to 12 minutes, until the kale is wilted and soft. Transfer to a serving bowl.

While the kale is steaming, whisk together the orange juice, ginger, and tahini. Season with salt. Add to the bowl and toss with the kale to coat. Sprinkle with sesame seeds and serve.

YIELD: 4 servings

NORI ROASTED POTATOES

USA

JAPAN

A little ground-up nori adds a fusion zing (not to mention lots of B vitamins!) to otherwise boring roasted potatoes.

1 tablespoon (9 g) garlic powder

1 tablespoon (8 g) ground toasted nori flakes (two sheets toasted nori, ground in a dry food processor or coffee grinder)

1 teaspoon dried dill

½ teaspoon dried parsley flakes

½ teaspoon onion powder

½ teaspoon sea salt, or to taste

¼ teaspoon chipotle powder or cayenne pepper

⅛ teaspoon ground cumin

⅛ teaspoon black pepper

1 tablespoon (15 g) prepared horseradish

¼ cup (60 ml) vegetable oil

2 pounds (908 g) russet potatoes, skin on, cut into bite-size chunks

Preheat the oven to 400°F (200°C, or gas mark 6). Line a baking sheet with parchment paper or a baking mat.

In a mixing bowl, whisk together all the ingredients except the potatoes. Add the potatoes to the bowl and toss to coat. Arrange in a single layer on the prepared baking sheet and bake for 25 to 30 minutes, tossing halfway through, until tender and golden brown.

YIELD: 4 servings

BLACK SESAME EDAMAME

Served hot or cold, this über-simple side is as tasty as it is quick!

3 tablespoons (45 ml) sesame oil

2 tablespoons (30 ml) soy sauce

2 teaspoons (6 g) black sesame seeds

4 cups (680 g) fully cooked shelled edamame

Whisk together the sesame oil, soy sauce, and sesame seeds. Add the edamame and toss to coat. Serve hot or cold.

YIELD: 4 servings

SWEET CHILE GREEN BEANS WITH MUSHROOMS

Try serving these green beans over rice or as a side to accompany the Hot, Sweet, and Sour Seitan Ribs with Lemongrass Bones (page 88), or chill them and add to your everyday leafy green salad.

2 tablespoons (30 ml) vegetable oil

1 shallot, thinly sliced

2 cloves garlic, thinly sliced

¼ cup (23 g) sliced almonds

½ cup (36 g) thinly sliced button mushrooms

1 pound (454 g) fresh green beans, trimmed

¼ cup (60 ml) Sweet Chile Sauce (page 21)

Heat the oil in a frying pan over medium heat. Add the shallot, garlic, and almonds. Sauté until fragrant and the almonds begin to turn toasty brown. Add the mushrooms and green beans and toss to coat. Cook for about 5 minutes, constantly tossing, until the mushrooms are soft and the beans are tender. Stir in the chile sauce and toss to coat, cook for 1 minute longer, and then serve.

YIELD: 4 servings

CHAPTER 6

WHET YOUR WHISTLE
ELIXIRS AND LIBATIONS

Sit back. Relax. Have a drink! Stay awhile. This chapter gives you plenty of reasons to invite a friend (or two, or ten) over for a fancy beverage. From healthy green smoothies to sassy sweet sippers, these recipes will have you shakin' up cocktails like a pro in no time.

FIZZY CILANTRO LIME JULEP

- Quick and Easy
- Soy Free
- Nut Free

MEXICO
USA

A Latin twist on a classic Southern cocktail!

2 tablespoons (2 g) fresh
   cilantro leaves
1 teaspoon sugar
juice from ½ lime
ice cubes
¼ cup (60 ml) bourbon
¼ cup (60 ml) club soda
wedge of lime, for garnish

Add the cilantro, sugar, and lime juice to the bottom of a cocktail glass and crush with a muddler. Pack the glass with ice and add the bourbon, then top with the club soda. Float a lime wedge on top.

YIELD: 1 serving

FUSION TIP

A muddler is a long, narrow, blunt tool, often shaped like a mini baseball bat, used to mash and muddle ingredients. If you don't have a muddler, you can use the handled end of a wooden spoon—the thicker, the better.

MATE MARGARITA

- Quick and Easy
- Soy Free

BRAZIL
MEXICO

Yerba mate packs a mean caffeine punch. And in this twist on a classic margarita, you can barely taste the alcohol, so be careful!

6 cups (1410 ml) brewed
   yerba mate, chilled
½ cup (120 ml) freshly
   squeezed lime juice
½ cup (120 ml) freshly
   squeezed orange juice
⅓ cup (112 g) agave nectar
1 cup (235 ml) Triple Sec
1½ cups (355 ml) silver tequila
lime wedges, for garnish
raw sugar, for garnish
ice cubes

In a large pitcher, stir together the yerba mate, lime juice, orange juice, agave, Triple Sec, and tequila. Wet the rim of a martini glass with a wedge of lime and dip the rim into a shallow bowl of sugar. Fill the glass with ice, pour the mixture over, and garnish with a wedge of lime.

YIELD: 3 quarts (2.8 L)

BANANA BLISS

○ **Quick and Easy**
○ **Soy Free**

Make a pitcher of this blended cocktail to serve up on movie night. I suggest a screening of *Beetlejuice* for the occasion.

USA
MEXICO

2 bananas
2 cups ice
1 cup (235 ml) Kahlúa
1 cup (235 ml) coconut water
¼ cup (60 ml) chocolate syrup
chocolate shavings, for garnish

Place the bananas, ice, Kahlúa, coconut water, and chocolate syrup in a blender and purée until smooth. Serve in a tall frosty mug. Garnish with a pinch of chocolate shavings.

YIELD: 2 servings

MANGO MADNESS

○ **Quick and Easy**
○ **Gluten Free**
○ **Soy Free**
○ **Nut Free**

This tropical smoothie is a refreshing summertime treat.

INDIA
THAILAND

1 cup (165 g) frozen mango chunks
1 banana
½ cup (90 g) frozen pineapple chunks
1 cup (235 ml) coconut water
1 cup (235 ml) pineapple juice

Add all the ingredients to a blender and blend until smooth. You can add a little more coconut water if your smoothie is too thick.

YIELD: 1 large smoothie

FUSION TIP

Are your bananas too ripe? Peel and freeze them. Frozen banana chunks are perfect for making smoothies!

ICED ALMOND COCONUT BUBBLE TEA

◉ Soy Free
◉ Nut Free

TAIWAN
USA

I love bubble tea, and will drive miles for it... And although the initial startup can be a bit time-consuming, as long as I keep a jar full of cooked tapioca bubbles in my fridge, I can make bubble tea whenever I want it!

For tapioca bubbles:

9 cups (2.1 L) water, divided

1 cup (152 g) white or brown tapioca pearls

1 cup (220 g) brown sugar, tightly packed

For almond coconut milk:

3 cups (705 ml) full-fat coconut milk

1 cup (235 ml) water

1 cup (200 g) granulated sugar

2 tablespoons (30 ml) almond extract

ice cubes

8 cups (2 L) strongly brewed black tea, chilled

8 bubble straws

To make the tapioca bubbles, fill a large pot with a lid with 8 cups (2 L) of water and bring to a rolling boil. Carefully add the tapioca pearls to the boiling water and stir to prevent them from sticking to the pot. Cover and boil for about 25 minutes. Uncover, remove from the heat, and let the tapioca sit in the water for another 25 minutes.

While the tapioca is cooking, bring the remaining 1 cup (235 ml) water to a boil, and stir in the brown sugar. Reduce to a simmer, and simmer until the sugar is completely dissolved, about a minute or two. Remove from the heat and allow to cool.

Rinse the cooked tapioca pearls in warm water and drain. Cover the rinsed tapioca pearls with the brown sugar syrup. Store the pearls in an airtight container in the refrigerator for up to 2 weeks.

To make the almond coconut milk, bring the coconut milk, water, and granulated sugar to a boil in a pot over medium-high heat. Reduce to a simmer, and stir to make sure all the sugar has dissolved. Remove from the heat, and stir in the almond extract. Allow to cool completely and store in an airtight container in the refrigerator for up to 2 weeks.

Assemble the drink in a 16-ounce (470 ml) glass. Start with a ¼-cup (28 g) scoop of bubbles in the bottom of the glass. Fill the glass with ice. Add 1 cup (235 ml) of black tea, and top off with the coconut almond milk. Serve with a wide bubble straw.

YIELD: 8 (16-ounce, or 470 ml) servings

TAMARINDO CON LECHE

This semisweet cocktail uses the paste from the ripened pod of the tamarind tree. This sweet, thick brown paste has many culinary uses. Try it in this cocktail for an interesting spin on a White Russian.

MEXICO
USA

1 tablespoon (15 g) tamarind paste

¼ cup (60 ml) vodka

½ cup (120 ml) coconut milk
   or other nondairy milk

1 tablespoon (15 ml) agave syrup

ice cubes

1 sprig mint, for garnish

Add the tamarind, vodka, coconut milk, agave, and ice to a cocktail shaker and shake vigorously. Pour into a cocktail glass and garnish with a sprig of mint.

YIELD: 1 serving

LEMON-LAVENDER GREEN TEA MARTINI

Soy Free
Nut Free

Classic cocktail buffs will absolutely cringe at the idea of calling this a martini. This pretty drink is a great summer cocktail and looks beautiful served in a punch bowl or large pitcher.

CHINA
USA

For simple syrup:

2 cups (470 ml) water

2 cups (400 g) sugar

2 lemons, sliced into rounds

½ cup (16 g) dried culinary lavender flowers

4 green tea bags

For cocktail:

1 part simple syrup

1 part gin

ice cubes

lemon wedge, for garnish

culinary lavender leaves, for garnish

To make the simple syrup, place all the ingredients in a pot and bring to a boil over medium-high heat. Boil until all the sugar is completely dissolved. Remove from the heat and allow to steep for at least 10 minutes and up to 1 hour.

Remove the tea bags and strain out the solids. Transfer the remaining syrup to an airtight container and store in the refrigerator until ready to use.

You can make a large pitcher or a single serving of this delicious drink. Just mix together equal parts syrup and gin, and serve over ice. Float a wedge of lemon and a pinch of lavender on top.

YIELD: 3 cups (705 ml) syrup

HOT TAMALE

Quick and Easy
Soy Free
Nut Free

This sweet and spicy cocktail will make you sweat! Serve it up alongside a big bowl of chips and guacamole at your next fiesta.

USA
MEXICO

2 slices fresh jalapeño pepper

2 tablespoons (2 g) fresh cilantro leaves

1 tablespoon (13 g) sugar

ice cubes

¼ cup (60 ml) gold tequila

¼ cup (60 ml) orange juice

¼ cup (60 ml) lemon lime soda

wedge of lime, for garnish

Place the jalapeño, cilantro, and sugar in the bottom of a cocktail glass and muddle (see page 130). Pack the glass with ice. Add the tequila and orange juice and top off with the lemon lime soda. Garnish with a wedge of lime.

YIELD: 1 serving

JAMAICA AGUA FRESCA

● Low Fat
● Gluten Free
● Soy Free
● Nut Free

MEXICO

Agua fresca is a traditional Mexican beverage usually made in large jars and includes fruit, sweetener, and water. They can be made with pretty much any kind of fruit, flower, cereal, or grain (like horchata, which is made with rice). This is one of my favorites!

3 quarts (3 L) water

1½ cups (75 g) dried Jamaica (hibiscus) flowers

1 tablespoon (6 g) minced fresh ginger

1½ cups (355 ml) agave syrup, or to taste

3 tablespoons (45 ml) fresh lime juice

1 large lime, thinly sliced into rounds

ice cubes

In a large pot, bring the water to a boil over high heat. Remove from the heat. Stir in the Jamaica flowers and ginger, and allow to steep for at least 10 minutes and up to 1 hour. Strain out the solids and stir in the agave, lime juice, and lime slices. Transfer to an ice-filled pitcher and serve.

YIELD: 3 quarts (3 L)

FUSION TIP

Spike it! Add ¼ cup (60 ml) vodka to your glass to make this an adult beverage.

MR. MIYAGI ➤

○ Quick and Easy
○ Nut Free

JAPAN
USA

Ever wonder how Mary got so bloody? Mr. Miyagi! Yeah, he seems so calm and collected, so Zen, so spiritual. But that sense of calm only came after he conquered his demons. His addiction to sake drenched in tomato juice and spicy Sriracha sauce made him wily and short-tempered. It is believed that it was he who burdened poor Mary with that dreaded moniker after a long night of drinking and debauchery in the back room of the bar that Mary tended. This left Mary to take the dreaded "walk of shame" before her coworkers, who could see the bloodshot, hungover look in her eyes. From that moment forward, she was known as Bloody Mary.

1 tablespoon (15 ml) soy sauce

½ teaspoon Sriracha sauce, or to taste

½ cup (120 ml) tomato juice

½ cup (120 ml) sake

ice cubes

1 scallion, optional, for garnish

1 slice jalapeño pepper, optional, for garnish

fresh cilantro, optional

freshly cracked black pepper to taste

Add the soy sauce, Sriracha, tomato juice, and sake to a shaker filled with ice. Shake vigorously and strain into a glass filled with ice. Garnish with freshly cracked pepper to taste, and optional scallion, jalapeño pepper, or cilantro.

YIELD: 1 serving

PINEAPPLE LYCHEE SAKE SANGRIA

○ Quick and Easy
○ Soy Free
○ Nut Free

JAPAN
PORTUGAL

This cocktail is just about as fusion as it gets! Try serving it up at your next sushi dinner party.

1 can (8 ounces, or 227 g) lychees in heavy syrup

1 can (15 ounces, or 420 g) crushed pineapple in juice

2½ cups (590 ml) sake

½ cup (120 ml) vodka

ice cubes

Remove the lychees from the syrup and chop into little pieces. Add the chopped lychees, syrup, crushed pineapple in juice, sake, and vodka to a large pitcher and stir to mix. Serve poured over ice.

YIELD: 2 quarts (2 L)

ICE-BLENDED MEXICAN HOT CHOCOLATE

○ **Quick and Easy**
○ **Soy Free**
○ **Nut Free**

USA
MEXICO

Step aside, Frappuccino, there is a new, grown-up ice-blended drink in town!

2 cups ice
1 cup (235 ml) Kahlúa
1 cup (235 ml) brewed coffee, chilled
1 cup (235 ml) full-fat coconut milk
¼ cup (60 ml) chocolate syrup
½ teaspoon cinnamon
cocoa powder, for garnish

Add the ice, Kahlúa, coffee, coconut milk, chocolate syrup, and cinnamon to a blender and purée until smooth. Divide between 2 large glasses. Sprinkle the top with a pinch of cocoa powder.

YIELD: 2 servings

SINGAPORE SUNRISE

- Quick and Easy
- Soy Free
- Nut Free

SINGAPORE
USA

This classy cocktail is a twist on the traditional Tequila Sunrise.

ice cubes

2 pieces lychees, packed in heavy syrup

2 tablespoons (30 ml) heavy syrup from the can of lychees

¼ cup (60 ml) vodka

¼ cup (60 ml) cranberry juice

¼ cup (60 ml) orange juice

twist of lime

Pack a cocktail glass with ice. Add the lychees, lychee syrup, vodka, and cranberry juice. Float the orange juice on top and finish with a twist of lime.

YIELD: 1 serving

MEXICAN MAI TAI

- Quick and Easy
- Nut Free
- Soy Free

MEXICO
USA

Make this sweet and festive drink at your next fusion taco party!

ice cubes

2 tablespoons (30 ml) silver tequila

¼ cup (60 ml) Kahlúa

½ cup (120 ml) pineapple juice

pineapple wedge, for garnish

Fill a glass with ice. Pour in the tequila and Kahlúa. Float pineapple juice on top. Garnish with a wedge of pineapple.

YIELD: 1 serving

IT'S NOT EASY BEING GREENS

- Quick and Easy
- Low Fat
- Gluten Free
- Soy Free
- Nut Free

USA
PHILLIPPINES

This green smoothie is not only full of fiber and nutrition from the veggies, but it actually tastes good, too! It's a great breakfast and a wonderful afternoon pick-me-up.

1 cup (30 g) baby spinach leaves
2 large leaves curly kale
1 cup (145 g) frozen blueberries
1 cup (180 g) frozen pineapple chunks
1 cup (235 ml) apple juice
1 cup (235 ml) coconut water

Add all the ingredients to a blender and purée until smooth. You can add extra apple juice or coconut water if your smoothie is too thick.

YIELD: 2 servings

FUSION TIP

Move over juice, green smoothies are in town! Did you know when you juice a vegetable or fruit you lose out on all of the fiber? By blending your fruits and veggies you are not only getting the whole food, but you are getting much needed fiber that can keep you feeling full longer, making smoothies a much more suitable meal replacement than a juice. Add in some silken tofu or your favorite protein powder to complete the meal.

CHAPTER 7

A SWEET FINISH
DESSERTS

Nothing completes a meal like a bite of rich, moist, decadent cake or cool, creamy, homemade ice cream. This final chapter contains out-of-the-ordinary desserts filled with extraordinary flavors like ginger, beet, avocado, chile, and curry. Transforming everyday desserts into something very memorable … now, that is something I can get behind.

SESAME COCONUT SQUARES

INDIA
USA

Super easy and quick, these sweet little crunchy squares are so pretty with their festive black and white speckles. These treats travel well, too, so they are perfect to bring to parties and send to friends and loved ones in care packages.

2 cups (400 g) sugar

1 cup (235 ml) water

2 cups (240 g) finely shredded coconut

1 cup (128 g) sesame seeds (a mix of black and white is pretty, but either will do fine)

Line an 8 x 8-inch (20 x 20 cm) baking dish with parchment.

Add the sugar and water to a pot and bring to a boil over medium-high heat, stirring often to make sure the sugar gets dissolved. Continue to cook until the mixture reaches the soft ball stage, or 240°F (116°C) on a candy thermometer. Add the coconut and sesame seeds and stir to coat. Quickly transfer the mixture to the prepared pan and spread evenly, as it sets up quickly. Allow to cool completely before cutting into 2-inch (5 cm) squares.

YIELD: 16 pieces

SWEET RED BEAN PASTE

Red bean paste is a common ingredient in many Chinese desserts. There are many textures and sweeteners that can be achieved by switching up the way you do things. The recipe below is for a basic red bean paste that can be altered to suit your specific needs.

CHINA

2 cups (394 g) dry adzuki beans

6 cups (1410 ml) water

2 cups (400 g) sugar

Sort and rinse the beans. Place in a bowl, cover with water, and soak overnight.

Rinse the soaked beans, place in a pot, and cover with the 6 cups (1.4 L) fresh water. Bring to a boil over medium-high heat, and then reduce to a simmer. Simmer for 45 minutes to 1 hour, or until tender. Drain the beans and return them to the pot. Add the sugar and mash until smooth. You can also do this in a food processor or blender.

YIELD: 3½ cups (990 g)

FUSION TIP

Here are three alternative methods of preparation.

· After rinsing the soaked beans, add the sugar and beans to the pot, cover with the 6 cups (1.4 L) fresh water, and simmer for 1 hour. This results in sweeter beans.

· After simmering the beans, drain and then press through a sieve to remove the skins of the beans. This results in a smoother, silkier paste.

· Add a small amount of oil when mashing the beans. This results in a smoother paste.

RED BEAN MODAK

Sweet red bean paste is a popular ingredient in Chinese desserts, such as mochi. Modak is an Indian dessert made from rice flour and usually stuffed with a blend of coconut, jaggery, and other flavorings. It seemed so natural to mix the two together.

2 ½ cups (590 ml) water

1 teaspoon vegetable oil, plus more for coating

½ teaspoon salt

3 cups (360 g) rice flour

1 cup (280 g) Sweet Red Bean paste (page 147)

Bring the water, 1 teaspoon oil, and salt to a boil in a saucepan over medium-high heat. As soon as the water begins to boil, remove from the heat. Carefully remove 1 cup (235 ml) of the water and reserve for later use. Slowly stir in the rice flour, ¼ cup (30 g) at a time, stirring constantly to prevent lumps. Eventually, the spoon will no longer be effective, and you will need to knead the dough. The consistency should be like soft Play-Doh. Add the reserved hot water as needed.

Divide the dough into sixteen pieces, about the size of a golf ball, and roll into balls. Coat each ball in a small amount of oil. Oil your hands and flatten one ball. Add 1 tablespoon (18 g) red bean paste to the center, wrap the dough around the paste, seal, and smooth the ball. If you have a cookie stamp, this is a fun way to use it, by pressing a design into the top of the ball. Repeat with the remaining dough and red bean paste.

Place the balls in a single layer in a steamer and steam for 20 minutes. Allow to cool completely before serving.

YIELD: 16 balls

SWEET ORANGE BASIL CURD

THAILAND
USA

This sweet curd is just divine over a bowl of fresh berries!

¼ cup (60 ml) coconut oil

1 cup (200 g) sugar

1½ cups (355 ml) almond
   milk, divided

½ cup (120 ml) freshly
   squeezed orange juice

zest of 1 orange

¼ cup (32 g) cornstarch

2 teaspoons (10 ml) vanilla extract

5 large leaves fresh basil chiffonade

Add the coconut oil, sugar, 1 cup (235 ml) of the almond milk, orange juice, and zest to a pot. The orange juice will curdle with the almond milk. That is okay; it will come back together once the slurry is added. Stir to combine, and bring to a boil over medium-high heat, stirring often.

In a separate bowl, mix together the cornstarch and remaining ½ cup (120 ml) almond milk to make a slurry. Slowly add the slurry to the boiling mixture and stir for 1 to 2 minutes, until thickened. Once thickened, remove from the heat. Stir in the vanilla and basil. Let cool completely. The curd will continue to thicken as it cools.

YIELD: 4 servings

AVOCADO LIME TARTLETS WITH SHORTBREAD CRUST

USA
MEXICO

These tarts are sweet, creamy, and green from the rich, buttery avocados.

For crust:

½ cup (115 g) firmly packed brown sugar

1 cup (224 g) nondairy butter or coconut oil

¼ teaspoon salt

2 ¼ cups (270 g) all-purpose flour, divided

For filling:

4 ripe avocados, peeled and pitted

1 can (15 ounces, or 420 g) coconut cream

½ cup (120 ml) lime juice 4 ounces (113 g) extra-firm tofu, drained

1 teaspoon apple cider vinegar

1 teaspoon vanilla extract

zest of 1 lime, plus extra for garnish

2 cups (240 g) powdered sugar, or as needed

½ cup (60 g) sweetened coconut shreds or flakes

To make the crust, preheat the oven to 325°F (170°C, or gas mark 3). Using an electric mixer, cream together the brown sugar and butter. Add the salt and mix to combine. Add 2 cups (240 g) of the flour and mix well. Turn the mixture out onto a floured work surface and knead for about 5 minutes, adding the remaining ¼ cup (30 g) flour as needed.

Press about ¼ cup (56 g) of the dough into the bottom of a cupcake tin, press firmly to create a "bowl" or you can use mini pie tins, tart pans, or even one of those dessert cup pans.

Bake the tart crusts for 20 to 25 minutes, or until golden. Cool before removing from the pan.

To make the filling, add the avocados, coconut cream, lime juice, tofu, vinegar, vanilla, and lime zest to the bowl of a mixer. Mix until smooth. Add the powdered sugar, ½ cup (60 g) at a time, and continue to mix until fully incorporated. The texture should be silky and thick, like custard. If yours is still too runny, you can add more sugar, ¼ cup (30 g) at a time. Sometimes, an electric mixer just can't make the really smooth, almost whipped consistency that you are after, so I finish the job off with my immersion blender. The texture should be that of a thick pudding or custard. Refrigerate until ready to use.

In a dry pan, toast the coconut flakes until lightly browned, and set aside.

Pipe the filling into the cooled tart shells. Sprinkle each with extra lime zest and toasted coconut.

YIELD: 6 to 12 tarts, depending on size

MEXICANNOLI

● Nut Free

MEXICO

ITALY

Looking for the perfect dessert to serve on Mexican food night? Roll these on for size. Light and crispy and sweet, these giant cannoli are the perfect way to end a Latin-inspired meal.

For filling:

½ cup (112 g) nondairy butter or coconut oil

6 ounces (170 g) extra-firm tofu, drained and pressed

1 teaspoon ground cinnamon

½ teaspoon ground cardamom

1 teaspoon vanilla extract

5 cups (600 g) powdered sugar

For cannoli shells:

vegetable oil, for frying

1 cup (200 g) granulated sugar

¼ teaspoon ground cinnamon

8 medium-size (8 inches, or 20 cm) flour tortillas

To make the filling, cream the butter and tofu together in the bowl of your stand mixer. Add the cinnamon, cardamom, and vanilla and continue to beat. Add the powdered sugar, 1 cup (120 g) at a time. Beat until fluffy, cover, and store in the refrigerator until ready to use.

To make the cannoli shells, pour the oil into a frying pan or skillet to a depth of ½ inch (1.3 cm) and heat over high heat to 350°F (180°C), or until a piece of tortilla dropped into the oil sizzles immediately.

While the oil is heating, mix together the sugar and cinnamon in a large shallow dish. Set aside. Line 2 plates with paper towels.

Roll up a tortilla so that the opening on each end is about 1 inch (2.5 cm) in diameter. Hold the tortilla's shape with tongs and place in the oil to fry for about 7 to 10 seconds, then carefully roll to fry evenly on all sides. Transfer to the paper towel–lined plate to quickly drain excess oil, and then immediately place in the sugar and cinnamon mixture to coat. Transfer to a second plate to cool completely. Repeat with the remaining tortillas and sugar-cinnamon mixture, bringing the oil back up to temperature after each one.

Using a piping bag and your largest star piping tip, pipe the filling into each end of the cannoli shell so that a tiny bit pops out of the end.

YIELD: 8 Mexicannoli

MANDARIN ORANGE BUNDT CAKE

• Nut Free

CHINA

USA

This moist cake is not overly sweet, and therefore, I find it perfectly appropriate to eat for breakfast!

3 cups (360 g) all-purpose flour

1 tablespoon (8 g) cornstarch

1 teaspoon baking powder

½ teaspoon baking soda

½ teaspoon salt

6 ounces (170 g) soft silken tofu, puréed

1 cup (200 g) sugar

1 can (15 ounces, or 420 g) mandarin oranges in light syrup, divided

1 teaspoon vanilla extract

½ cup (120 ml) full-fat coconut milk

¼ cup (60 ml) vegetable oil

2 tablespoons (12 g) orange zest, divided

⅔ cup (80 g) powdered sugar

2 tablespoons (30 ml) orange juice

Preheat the oven to 350°F (180°C, or gas mark 4). Grease a standard Bundt pan.

In a large mixing bowl, mix together the flour, cornstarch, baking powder, baking soda, and salt.

In a separate bowl, mix together the tofu, sugar, 1 cup (235 ml) of the syrup from the mandarin oranges (reserve the orange segments for later use), vanilla, coconut milk, oil, and 1 tablespoon (6 g) of the orange zest. Add the wet mixture to the dry and stir to combine. Do not overmix.

Mince the orange segments, and fold into the batter. Pour the batter into the Bundt pan. Bake for 45 to 55 minutes, or until a toothpick inserted near the center comes out clean. Remove from the oven. Allow to cool and then invert onto a serving plate.

In a small bowl, whisk together the powdered sugar and orange juice until smooth. Drizzle all over the cake. Sprinkle the remaining 1 tablespoon (6 g) orange zest over the top.

YIELD: 1 standard Bundt cake

CHURROS WITH SWEET COCONUT CREAM FILLING

Churros are the one thing I thought for sure I'd have to give up when I went vegan. I never even considered how easy it is to make these bad boys at home! Now it's perfectly okay to skip the filling and just get your churro on, but just promise me that one day you will try it stuffed with the sweet cream, okay?

For churros:

2 cups (470 ml) water

¼ cup (50 g) granulated sugar

1 teaspoon salt

¼ cup (60 ml) vegetable oil, plus more for frying

2 cups (240 g) all-purpose flour

For cinnamon sugar coating:

½ cup (100 g) granulated sugar

1 teaspoon ground cinnamon

For filling:

¼ cup (60 ml) coconut cream

1 cup (120 g) powdered sugar, or as needed

1 teaspoon ground cinnamon

To make the churros, in a small pot over medium heat, add the water, granulated sugar, salt, and ¼ cup (60 ml) oil. Bring to a boil and then remove from the heat. Vigorously stir in the flour until the mixture comes together into a soft ball.

If you have a deep fryer, this is a great time to use it. If not, a pot filled with 4 inches (10 cm) of oil heated to 350°F (180°C) will work perfectly.

Add the dough to a large pastry bag (you may have to do this in 2 batches) fitted with a very large star tip. Pipe strips of dough about 4-inches (10 cm) long into the oil. Fry for about 2 to 3 minutes, or until golden and crispy. Transfer to a plate lined with paper towels to absorb excess oil.

To make the coating, mix together the sugar and cinnamon in a shallow dish. Toss the churros in the mixture to coat while they are still warm. Enjoy as is, or proceed to the next step to fill them.

To make the filling, beat together all the ingredients with an electric mixer until the consistency of frosting. Using a piping bag with a filling tip, pipe the filling into the center of the churro, once it is cooled.

YIELD: 16 pieces

COCONUT GINGER BEET ICE CREAM

● Nut Free | This bright pink ice cream gets its color from the beets and has a little bite from the ginger.

USA
THAILAND

1 cup (235 ml) water

1 medium red beet, peeled
and chopped

2 tablespoons (12 g) minced
fresh ginger

2 cups (470 ml) full-fat coconut milk

2 cups (400 g) sugar

¼ cup (32 g) cornstarch

scrapings from 1 vanilla bean

1 teaspoon vanilla extract

1 cup (120 g) finely shredded coconut

2 tablespoons (30 ml) lemon juice

Add the water, beet, and ginger to a blender and purée until smooth. Add the puréed mixture to a saucepan, along with the coconut milk, sugar, cornstarch, and the scrapings from the vanilla bean. Stir to combine.

Bring to a boil, stirring often. As soon as it begins to boil, remove from the heat and stir in the vanilla extract, shredded coconut, and lemon juice. Place in the refrigerator to cool for an hour or so, then follow the instructions for your ice cream maker (or see tip).

YIELD: Just over 4 cups (600 g)

FUSION TIP

Although we all scream for ice cream, we also know that not everyone has access to an ice cream maker. Here are some simple instructions (although a bit more laborious) to make delicious homemade ice cream without one. The purpose of an ice cream maker is to aerate the ice cream and prevent it from becoming too crystallized as it freezes. This can be accomplished with an electric mixer, as long as you have a few hours to spend. Don't worry. Most of that time is downtime. After making the ice cream mixture, pour it into a mixing bowl and chill in the refrigerator for 2 hours, then place it in the freezer for about 30 minutes. Remove it from the freezer and beat with a mixer until creamy. Put back into the freezer for another 30 minutes. Repeat this process three times before placing it in the freezer for the final freeze, usually overnight, for a nice, firm ice cream.

CURRY MANGO CRISPY PIE BITES

Now I don't advocate eating these every day, but these little buggers sure do make a nice treat every now and again! I mean, they are deep-fried and then dipped in a sugary glaze—what's not to love?

vegetable oil, for frying

1 package (1 pound, or 454 g) vegan puff pastry

1 cup (165 g) mango chunks (frozen is fine)

½ cup (100 g) granulated sugar

¼ cup (36 g) currants or raisins

1 teaspoon yellow curry powder

2 tablespoons (30 ml) lemon juice

2 cups (240 g) powdered sugar

¼ cup (60 ml) coconut or other nondairy milk

If you have a deep fryer, this is a great time to use it. If not, a pot filled with 4 inches (10 cm) of oil heated to 350°F (180°C) will work perfectly.

Thaw puff pastry according to package instructions.

Add the mango, granulated sugar, currants, curry, and lemon juice to a pot. Heat over medium heat until the sugar has melted and the mangos are soft and syrupy. Remove from the heat and set aside to cool.

Cut the sheet of puff pastry into 16 rectangles measuring approximately 5 x 3 inches (12.5 x 7.5 cm). Create a pocket by folding one rectangle in half and sealing the two outer edges with the tines of a fork, leaving an opening at the top. Add 1 heaping tablespoon (28 g) of the mango mixture to the pocket, and seal the opening with the tines of a fork. Repeat with the remaining pieces.

Add 2 pie bites at a time to the oil and fry for about 1 to 1½ minutes, then carefully flip and cook an additional 1 to 1½ minutes, or until puffy, golden, and crispy. Transfer to a plate lined with paper towels to absorb excess oil. Repeat until all 16 pie bites are fried.

In a small bowl, whisk together the powdered sugar and coconut milk until smooth. Dip each pie bite into the glaze and place on a wire rack to cool and dry completely. Be sure to place a kitchen towel or paper towels underneath your rack to catch the dripping glaze.

YIELD: 16 pie bites

SESAME PINE NUT BRITTLE

Gluten Free

USA

JAPAN

A candy thermometer is super helpful in this recipe. If you don't have one, you can test for doneness by dropping a teaspoon full of the boiling mixture into a bowl of ice water; if it immediately forms into a hard ball, it's ready.

nonstick cooking spray

2 cups (240 g) pine nuts

2 tablespoons (16 g) black sesame seeds

2 cups (400 g) sugar

1 cup (235 ml) light corn syrup

1 cup (235 ml) water

½ teaspoon salt

2 tablespoons (28 g) nondairy butter

1 tablespoon (15 ml) vanilla extract

1 teaspoon baking soda

Have ready a rimmed baking sheet lined with parchment and sprayed liberally with nonstick spray.

In a saucepan, mix together the pine nuts, sesame seeds, sugar, corn syrup, water, and salt. Place over low heat, and stir until the sugar has melted. Raise the heat to high and bring to a boil. Continue to boil until it reaches 300°F (150°C) on a candy thermometer.

Meanwhile, mix together the butter, vanilla, and baking soda in a separate bowl.

Once the boiling mixture reaches 300°F (150°C), remove from the heat and vigorously stir in the butter mixture. It will foam and fizz. Quickly pour the mixture onto the baking sheet and spread evenly. Allow to cool completely before breaking into pieces and enjoying. Store in an airtight container lined with waxed paper.

YIELD: About 40 pieces

MEXICAN HOT CHOCOLATE CAKE TRUFFLES

These sweet, rich, and just a tad spicy truffles are a perfect alternative to cupcakes!

MEXICO
USA

For cake:

3 cups (360 g) all-purpose flour

⅔ cup (80 g) cocoa powder

2 teaspoons baking soda

1 teaspoon salt

1 heaping teaspoon cinnamon

2 cups (470 ml) water

2 cups (400 g) sugar

½ cup plus 2 tablespoons (150 ml) vegetable oil

2 teaspoons vanilla extract

2 tablespoons (30 ml) apple cider vinegar

For ganache:

½ cup (120 ml) full-fat coconut cream

1 cup (176 g) vegan chocolate chips

1 tablespoon (15 ml) chocolate extract

¼ teaspoon chipotle powder

For chocolate coating:

4 cups (704 g) vegan chocolate chips

1 tablespoon (6 g) ground cinnamon, divided

1 teaspoon chipotle powder

To make the cake, preheat the oven to 350°F (180°C, or gas mark 4). Coat a 9 x 12-inch (23 x 30 cm) baking pan with nonstick spray. Mix the flour, cocoa powder, baking soda, salt, and cinnamon in a bowl. In a separate bowl, mix the water, sugar, oil, vanilla, and vinegar. Combine with the dry mixture. Pour into the prepared pan.

Bake for 40 to 50 minutes, until a toothpick inserted in the center comes out clean. Allow to cool to the touch.

To make the ganache, heat the coconut cream in a saucepan until it just begins to boil. Remove from the heat and stir in the chocolate chips, chocolate extract, and chipotle powder. Stir until melted and smooth. Allow to cool to the touch.

To make the truffles, in a large bowl, smash the cake with the ganache until well mixed and doughy. Form the dough into 1 heaping tablespoon (28 g) balls, and place on a cookie sheet lined with parchment. Insert a toothpick into each, and place in the freezer.

For the coating, melt the chocolate chips and 1 teaspoon (2 g) of the cinnamon in a double boiler. Once the balls are cold and firm, coat with the chocolate, using the toothpick as a handle. Return to the cookie sheet, remove the toothpick, and return to the freezer or refrigerator to harden.

Mix together 2 teaspoons (4 g) cinnamon and chipotle. Once the chocolate coating hardens, sprinkle with a pinch of the cinnamon-chipotle mixture. Place in a cupcake paper to serve!

YIELD: About 36 balls

COCONUT TRES LECHES CAKE

USA
MEXICO

This cake strays a bit from what most people are used to when it comes to a tres leches cake, because in this cake, we are only going to use coconut milk, but in three ways: in the form of milk, yogurt, and an evaporated sweet glaze.

For cake:

1 ½ cups (180 g) all-purpose flour

1 cup (120 g) sweetened
   coconut flakes

2 tablespoons (18 g) cornstarch

½ teaspoon baking soda

½ teaspoon baking powder

¼ teaspoon salt

1 cup (200 g) sugar

¼ cup (60 ml) coconut oil, melted

3 ounces (85 g) plain or
   vanilla coconut yogurt

¼ cup (60 g) puréed silken tofu

½ cup (120 ml) full-fat coconut milk

1 teaspoon vanilla extract

For glaze:

2 cups (470 ml) full-fat coconut milk

1 cup (200 g) sugar

To make the cake, preheat the oven to 350°F (180°C, or gas mark 4). Spray a 9-inch (23 cm) round cake pan with nonstick spray or line with parchment paper.

In a large mixing bowl, mix together the flour, coconut, cornstarch, baking soda, baking powder, and salt.

In a separate large bowl, mix together the sugar, oil, yogurt, tofu, coconut milk, and vanilla. Add the wet mixture to the dry and stir until smooth, taking care not to overmix. Spread the batter evenly in the cake pan. Bake for 35 to 40 minutes, until golden and a toothpick inserted into the center comes out clean.

To make the glaze, in a pot, mix together the coconut milk and sugar. Bring to a boil over medium-high heat, lower the heat to a simmer, and simmer until the mixture is reduced by half, 5 to 7 minutes.

Remove the cake from the oven and allow to cool for 10 minutes. Invert onto a rimmed cake plate or a 9-inch (23 cm) pie tin. You will need to make sure there is something to catch the extra glaze. Poke holes all over the top of the cake with a fork. Slowly pour the coconut glaze all over the cake so that it absorbs into the cake and pools around the bottom.

YIELD: One 9-inch (23 cm) cake

FUSION TIP:

You can top this cake with extra coconutty goodness by toasting 1 cup (120 g) shredded coconut in a very dry pan over medium heat until slightly browned, and then sprinkling it all over the cake.

ORANGE ALMOND TOFU CRÈME BRÛLÉE

This classic dessert is sure to please even the pickiest of sugar lovers.

¼ cup (28 g) raw cashew pieces

8 ounces (227 g) soft silken tofu, drained

½ cup (120 ml) coconut cream

¾ cup (150 g) sugar, divided

1 tablespoon (15 ml) almond extract

1 tablespoon (15 ml) orange extract

¼ cup (23 g) sliced almonds

zest from 1 orange

Soak the cashews covered in water overnight. Drain and rinse before using.

Preheat the oven to 350°F (180°C, or gas mark 4).

Add the soaked cashews, tofu, coconut cream, ½ cup (100 g) of the sugar, and the extracts to a blender and purée until smooth. Pour the mixture evenly into four 3-inch (7.5 cm) ramekins. Place the ramekins in a baking pan and fill the pan with water so that it comes halfway up the sides of the ramekins. The purpose of this step is to add moisture to the oven and prevent your desserts from cracking on the top.

Carefully place the pan in the oven and bake for 45 minutes. The brûlées should rise similarly to that of a soufflé and then they will shrink back down after cooling.

Carefully remove the pan from the oven, and carefully remove the ramekins from the pan. Allow them to cool completely before topping.

While cooling, mix together the remaining ¼ cup (50 g) sugar, sliced almonds, and orange zest.

Once the brûlées are cool, sprinkle an equal amount of the sugar mixture evenly over the top of each dessert. Caramelize the tops either by using a kitchen torch, sweeping slowly side to side until browned, or by placing the ramekins beneath a preheated broiler and watching closely. Remove from the broiler as soon as the tops begin to brown. Serve immediately, so that the sugar topping stays hard and crispy.

YIELD: 4 servings

KEY LIME COCONUT CREAM PIE

USA
THAILAND

I think the name pretty much says it all with this dreamy dessert! There are two ways to make it: stove top or oven baked. The stove top version is lighter and tangier, while the oven-baked version is richer and creamier. Both are delicious.

2 cups (470 ml) coconut
cream, divided

¾ cup (180 ml) Key lime juice

1 cup (200 g) sugar

¼ cup (32 g) arrowroot powder

1 tablespoon (15 ml) vanilla extract

1 block (12 ounces, or 340 g) soft silken
tofu, for oven-baked method only

1 shortbread pie crust (page 152)

¾ cup (90 g) shredded coconut,
toasted (see tip, page 162)

zest from 2 Key limes

For the stove top method, add 1½ cups (355 ml) of the coconut cream, lime juice, and sugar to a pot and bring to a boil. In a separate bowl, mix together the arrowroot powder and remaining ½ cup (120 ml) coconut cream to make a slurry and set aside.

As soon as the mixture begins to boil, remove from the heat. Stir in the arrowroot slurry and stir until it thickens. Add the vanilla and continue to stir. Immediately pour into the pie crust and refrigerate for at least 2 hours, preferably overnight, to cool and set. Top with the toasted coconut and lime zest.

For the oven-baked method, preheat the oven to 350°F (180°C, or gas mark 4).

Add the coconut cream, lime juice, sugar, arrow-root powder, vanilla, and tofu to a blender and purée until smooth. Pour into the crust and place on a baking sheet (to protect your oven). Bake for 1 hour, or until the filling is bubbly.

Remove from the oven and place in the refrigerator to completely cool and set. Top with the toasted coconut and lime zest.

YIELD: One 9-inch (23 cm) pie

FUSION TIP

The shortbread crust for the Avocado Lime Tartlet (page 152) is perfect for this pie. Or, you can make a crustless version by following the oven-baked method and pouring the filling directly into individual ramekins.

ACKNOWLEDGMENTS
WHAT WOULD I DO WITHOUT YOU?

This book would simply never have been written if it weren't for the selfless efforts of the extraordinary team of testers from around the globe! These amazing folks volunteer their time, talents, and kitchens to test, retest, and give honest feedback on each and every recipe in this book! I would like to extend an amazing amount of gratitude and love to the following testers:

Dawn Carlock, who blogs at veganfazool.blogspot.com and tweets @VeganFazool. Her favorite fusion trick has been using the Barbecue Bun Pull-Apart Bread recipe (page 36) and stuffing it with different ingredients, then dipping it in various dipping sauces! She says each variant has come out really well, including vegan "calzone bites" that she and her husband developed, and dipped in their own CSA garlic-infused marinara!

Dorothy Mora, whose favorite tip is that there are so many ways to personalize these recipes! She's had so much fun changing out ingredients or using different sauces. Her second tip would be that the sauces freeze well—for example, she thawed a container of Hot, Sweet, and Sour Sauce (page 25) while preparing the bean balls. Her favorite ingredients from these recipes are citrus and garlic.

Kelly Reckas, who blogs at kohlrabiandquince.wordpress.com and tweets @kellycrochets. Her favorite fusion ingredient is chipotle. She loves that the smoky spiciness goes well with everything from chickpeas to chocolate. Her best fusion cooking tip? Don't be afraid to seek out new ingredients or new flavor combinations. Some of her favorite meals have come out of mystery farmers' market finds.

Livvie Allman, whose favorite fusion ingredient would have to be garlic. She loves it, and it can go in anything savory.

Kim Lahn, who blogs at kimcooksveg4u.blogspot.com. She says it's hard to pick a favorite fusion ingredient, but she does love all chiles, Sriracha, and miso!

Sarah Mercush, who blogs at imnotstarving.blogspot.com. Her favorite fusion-y ingredient is cilantro—anything that you can add cilantro to should have it: Tex-Mex, Indian, it all works! As for her favorite fusion-y technique? Don't be afraid of mixing foods—you have to try different things together to see how they work. Also, sometimes if she's making a few things that don't quite "match," flavor profile wise, she adds some of the herbs and spices from one dish into the other, just to get them a little more in line with each other.

Liz Wyman, who blogs at cookingtheveganbooks.com. Her favorite fusion ingredients are sesame seeds, oil, tahini, and sesame paste: "Yum to it all."

Alisha Moses, who blogs at www.zombiesatemy sandwiches.wordpress.com. Her favorite fusion ingredients are Sriracha because of its unique flavor and intense heat. It tastes great on everything!

Sara Luckett, whose fusion tip is to use what you have on hand. Some of her best "fusion" recipes were not planned, but the result of being too lazy (or budget-minded) to get what she would normally use or what the recipe called for.

Sara Rose, whose favorite fusion ingredient is cumin. She loves its unique flavor in everything from Indian curry to Tex-Mex salsa.

Kelly Cavalier, whose favorite fusion ingredient is hard to pick, but she would have to go with citrus. You can use it in sweet or savory dishes and it always adds a little something to any dish. Plus, it is used in so many different cuisines that it can definitely cross borders while you are mixing and matching flavors.

Christy Beauregard, whose favorite fusion ingredient is GARLIC! It's enjoyed by many cultures and adds so much flavor. Yum.

Rachel Strasser, who blogs at madeleineteacup. com and tweets @madelaineteacup. Her favorite fusion ingredient is ginger. After all, it is very well traveled (India! China! Japan! Korea! Finland!) and

can be used in a main dish or a dessert, as a foodstuff or a beverage, in sweet or savory applications. A rhizome of all trades!

Erin Goddard, who blogs at meet-the-wikos.com. Her favorite fusion ingredient is probably sambal oelek. It tastes like much more than the sum of its parts, and adds something special that you can't quite put your finger on.

Kelly Williams, who blogs at vegga.wordpress. com. She loves the versatility of peanut sauce—you can do so much with it, and it complements all sorts of meals!

Stephanie Stansby, who blogs at thecraftykitty. co.uk. She has really come around to Sriracha, which she never thought would happen! She is a chile-phobe, and found that she just can't stop making the Sloppy Joe Pho (page 73) and the Creamy Sesame Sriracha Sauce (page 16). She'll put that sauce on everything now!

Anna Holt (and sons!), who blog at finallywakingup wordpress.com and tweets @finallywakingup. Her favorite fusion ingredient is liquid smoke or chipotles because everything tastes better if it's smoky. Her favorite fusion cooking tip/trick is to reduce the chili/heat level in the recipes so that they are child-friendly. My boys loved everything we tried from this book, they like spice but not the heat (yet)!

MORE THANKS!

I would like to extend a heartfelt and sincere thank you to Amanda Waddell. Not only was it she who first took a chance on me, but it was also she who has continued to support me over the years despite my insane antics, missed deadlines, and frantic emails. Amanda has not only been there for me every step of the way, but she has also inspired me to be better and do better in this crazy world. Thank you, Amanda. I wouldn't be anywhere near where I am if it weren't for you!

Mr. Wade Hammond... there simply are no words. What a pleasure and a joy you have been to work with. Your pictures have elevated my cooking to whole new heights! You have an amazing eye, and a beautiful heart. This experience has been a wonderful one, and I hope we can continue to work together in the future.

Thanks, as well, to Michelle Thompson, Rachel Fitzgibbon, Katie Fawkes, Winnie Prentiss, Betsy Gammons, Karen Levy, and the rest of the amazing Fair Winds staff for putting together such a beautiful book. I am not exaggerating when I say that you guys make the most beautiful cookbooks, from the front cover to the last page of the index, in all the world. I know that all of you talented folks work so hard to make sure that each and every page is laid out and designed with such care and attention to detail, and for that I am grateful.

And, of course, a special thanks to Dan, for taking over my house chores while I followed right behind like a Tasmanian Devil, constantly making more messes in the kitchen; for walking the girls when I couldn't pull myself away from a recipe; and for waking me up to tell me to come to bed after I passed out on the couch. I love you with all of my heart and after eighteen years together, I can't believe I love you more and more, each and every day.

ABOUT THE AUTHOR

Six-time cookbook author Joni Marie Newman is just a regular gal who loves to cook, especially for friends and family. Self-taught, and still learning, she spends most of her time in the kitchen. When she's not in the kitchen, she really enjoys knitting, painting, wasting endless hours on the Internet, hiking with her husband and the girls, traveling, reading, and most of the other stuff regular gals enjoy. She currently resides in Orange County, California, in a small cottage, with her three rescued pups, and her extremely delicious husband, in one of the last rural towns in Southern California. It is in this cottage that she creates delicious and cruelty-free delicacies for the world to enjoy. Through her food, she hopes to help people understand that it is not necessary to murder or torture another living creature in order to have a tasty supper.

INDEX